# The Rights Revolution in the Twentieth Century

**Other Titles in this Series:**

*The War Power: Original and Contemporary*
by **Louis Fisher**

*Women and the U.S. Constitution, 1776–1920*
by **Jean H. Baker**

# The Rights Revolution in the Twentieth Century

by **Mark Tushnet**

**Published by the
American Historical Association
400 A Street, SE
Washington, D.C. 20003
www.historians.org**

MARK TUSHNET is the William Nelson Cromwell Professor of Law at Harvard Law School and the author of numerous works in constitutional theory and constitutional history, including *The NAACP's Legal Strategy against Segregated Education, 1925–50*; *Making Civil Rights Law: Thurgood Marshall and the Supreme Court, 1936–61*; *Making Constitutional Law: Thurgood Marshall and the Supreme Court, 1961–91*; and *A Court Divided: The Rehnquist Court and the Future of Constitutional Law.*

AHA EDITORS: David Darlington, Liz Townsend

LAYOUT: Chris Hale

The New Essays on Constitutional History series is also sponsored by the Institute for Constitutional History at the New-York Historical Society, and the George Washington University Law School.

© 2009 by the American Historical Association
ISBN: 978-0-87229-165-2

Published in 2009 by the American Historical Association. As publisher, the American Historical Association does not adopt official views on any field of history and does not necessarily agree or disagree with the views expressed in this book.

Library of Congress Cataloging-in-Publication Data

Tushnet, Mark V., 1945–

The rights revolution in the twentieth century / By Mark Tushnet.
    p. cm. -- (New essays on American constitutional history)
Includes bibliographical references and index.
ISBN 978-0-87229-165-2 (alk. paper)
1. Civil rights--United States--History--20th century. I. Title.
KF4749.T87 2009      342.7308'50904--dc      222009021186

# Table of Contents

# Series Introduction

ew Essays on American Constitutional History is published by the American Historical Association, in association with the Institute for Constitutional Studies. This series follows the lead of its predecessor, the Bicentennial Essays on the Constitution, published by the AHA under the editorship of Herman Belz as part of the commemoration of the two hundredth anniversary of the Constitution over two decades ago. The goal remains the same. The essays are intended to provide both students and teachers with brief, accessible, and reliable introductions to some of the most important aspects of American constitutional development. The essays reflect the leading scholarship in the field and address topics that are classic, timely, and always important.

American constitutionalism is characterized by a series of tensions. Such tensions are persistent features of American constitutional history, and they make a frequent appearance in these essays. The American tradition emphasizes the importance of written constitutions. The United States Constitution declares that "this Constitution" is the "supreme law of the land." But time moves on. Politics and society are ever changing. How do we manage the tension between being faithful to a written constitutional text and adapting to changing political circumstances? To the extent that the American brand of constitutionalism binds us to the past, creates stability, and slows political change, how do we balance these conservative forces with the pressures of the moment that might demand departures from inherited ways of doing things and old ideas about rights and values? We sometimes change the terms of the old text through amendment or wholesale replacement of one constitution with another (from the Articles of Confederation to the Constitution at the national level, or more often at the state level), but we apply and adapt the inherited constitutional text through interpretation and practice. All the while, we manage the tension between being faithful to the text that we have and embracing the "living constitution" that grows out of that text.

Law figures prominently in the American constitutional tradition. Our written constitutions are understood to be fundamental laws and part of our legal code. They are the foundation of our legal system and superior to all other laws. They provide legally enforceable rules for judges and others to follow. Judges and lawyers play an important role in interpreting American constitutions and translating the bare bones of the original text into the detailed body of doctrine known as constitutional law. It has often been the dream of judges, lawyers, and legal scholars to insulate constitutional law from the world of politics. There is a long-held aspiration for judges and lawyers to be able to spin out constitutional law in accord with established principles of justice, reason, and tradition. But politics has also been central to the history of American constitutionalism. Constitutions are created by political actors and serve political purposes. Once in place, constitutional rules and values are politically contested, and they are interpreted and put into practice by politicians and political activists, as well as by judges. The tension between law and politics is a persistent one in American constitutional history.

A final tension of note has been between power and liberty. In the modern tradition, constitutional government is limited government. Constitutions impose limits and create mechanisms for making those constraints effective. They specify what the boundaries of government power are and what rights individuals and groups have against government. But there is also an older tradition, in which constitutions organize and empower government. The U.S. Constitution contains both elements. Many of its provisions, especially the amendments, limit government. These are some of the most celebrated features of the Constitution, and they have become the basis for much of the constitutional law that has been developed by the judiciary. But the Constitution was specifically adopted to empower the federal government and create new, better institutions that could accomplish national objectives. Both the U.S. Constitution and the state constitutions are designed to gather and direct government power to advance the public good. Throughout American constitutional history, judges, politicians, and activists have struggled over the proper balance between empowering government and limiting government and over the best understanding of the rights of individuals and the public welfare.

These essays examine American constitutionalism, not a particular constitutional text. The U.S. Constitution figures prominently in these essays, as it does in American history, but the American constitutional tradition includes other foundational documents, including notably the state constitutions. These texts are a guide to the subject matter of these essays, but they are not exhaustive of it. Laws, court decisions, administrative actions, and custom, along with founding documents, perform constitutional functions in the American political system, just as they do in the British system where there is no single written "constitution." Whether "written" or "unwritten," constitutions perform certain common tasks. Constitutions define the organic structures of government, specifying the basic institutions for making and implementing public policy, including the processes for altering the constitution itself. Constitutions distribute powers among those institutions of government, delegating, enumerating, prohibiting, and reserving powers to each governmental body. The flip side of entrusting power and discretion to governmental bodies is the definition of limits on those powers, the specification of individual and collective rights. Constitutions also specify who participates in the institutions of government and how and to whom the power of government applies. That is, constitutions identify the structures of citizenship and political jurisdiction. Across its seven articles and twenty-seven amendments, the U.S. Constitution addresses all of these topics, but the text is only a starting point. These topics form the subject matter of New Essays on American Constitutional History.

Writing early in the twentieth century, the great constitutional historian Edward Corwin observed that relatively few citizens actually read the U.S. Constitution, despite its brevity. He thought that this was in part because the "real constitution of the United States has come to mean something very different from the document" itself. The document laid out the framework of government, but "the real scope of the powers which it should exercise and of the rights which it should guarantee was left, to a very great extent, for future developments to determine." Understanding American constitutionalism requires understanding American constitutional history. It is a history of contestation and change, creation and elaboration. These essays aim to illuminate that history.

—*Keith E. Whittington,*
*Princeton University*

—*Gerry Leonard,*
*Boston University School of Law*

# *Introduction*

he idea of rights has been central to U.S. political and constitutional discourse from the beginning. The Declaration of Independence appealed to "inalienable rights," and the first amendments to the Constitution were universally described as a bill of rights. Yet, something distinctive appears to have happened to the idea of rights over the course of the twentieth century. On most accounts, the 1960s and the Supreme Court under the leadership of Earl Warren and William Brennan marked the point of transformation. The Warren Court engaged in what came to be known as a revolution in criminal procedure, imposing high professional standards for police and prosecutors as a matter of constitutional law. The *Miranda* warnings became a part of popular culture, recited—and then sometimes ignored—on television shows and in film.[1] The Court consolidated and clarified free speech doctrines that had been emerging over the prior generation, with the effect of substantially expanding the protection afforded to libelous statements and sexually explicit material as well as political speech. Religious dissenters were protected against what they viewed as establishments of religion, and gained more robust protection for their activities under the Free Exercise Clause.

By the end of the century, rights claims were being asserted in locations, such as schools and prisons, where they had not been found at the century's beginning, and they were being asserted on behalf of claimants, such as fetuses and new arrivals to the United States, who were outside the domain of rights earlier. Even the content of rights claims changed. Much of the Warren Court's work completed a constitutional agenda outlined, albeit unclearly, in the 1940s and early 1950s as part of the New Deal's constitutional vindication. The Warren Court added something new—an emphasis on personal autonomy—to the New Deal's concerns for fairness in the political process.

Yet it would be misleading to describe the century as one in which the domain of rights "expanded" with no loss to society. New rights for some often mean fewer rights for others, and always mean that society's effort to achieve goals like prosperity and national security will be more difficult and costly. By the end of the century, some degree of reaction had set in, although its primary effect was to say, "Thus far and no more," leaving in place most of the Warren Court's work but refusing to extend it. And the Supreme Courts under Warren Burger and William Rehnquist actually did go farther than the Warren Court in giving constitutional protection to the right to choose with respect to abortion and to gay rights.

The idea of rights operates on several levels. Rights are part of U.S. culture, and part of political theory. On those levels, the idea of rights is sometimes quite abstract, and contradictions among the rights that are valued culturally and developed in theory can be quite persistent. Rights are brought home when they become *legal* rights. The changes in the idea of rights on which this essay focuses are changes on the level of law.

Changes occurred in *ideas* and *institutions*. Put simply, at the outset of the twentieth century, the prevailing idea of rights defined them with reference to the doctrines of classical liberalism with its emphasis on choice and contract in the market, supplemented by an ideal of equality expressed in hostility to class legislation that departed from neutral treatment of all groups in the economy and society. At the end of the century, rights were associated with a modern liberalism adding to the classical liberal account a concern for individual autonomy in all spheres of life, supplemented by a more substantive ideal of equality that extended, again, into all spheres of life. The changes can be captured in this way:

❖ In 1905, the Supreme Court used the doctrine of substantive due process to defend a liberty of contract against state regulation in *Lochner v. New York*; in 1965, the Court used the same doctrine to defend a freedom of choice with respect to sexual activity.[2]

❖ In 1905, *Lochner* found wage and hour legislation dealing with bakers unconstitutional because bakers were indistinguishable in constitutionally relevant respects from any other class of workers. In 1990, Congress enacted the Americans with Disabilities Act, which required accommodation of persons with disabilities, and though the scope of the required accommodations was controversial, the requirement of accommodation—an expression of an ideal of substantive equality, here as between those with disabilities and those without—was not.

❖ In 1896, *Plessy v. Ferguson* sharply distinguished between civil rights, a limited class of rights enjoyed by everyone without regard to race, and social rights, a broader class attached to the ordinary activities of everyday life, as to which racial equality was not required.³ The Civil Rights Act of 1964, using the old term, insisted on racial equality with respect to what earlier would have been called social rights.

The institutional changes over the course of the twentieth century had three main components. First, and the most limited, was the development of networks of lawyers whose primary work involved efforts to vindicate constitutional rights. Starting with what legal historian Daniel Ernst described as "lawyers against labor," these networks expanded dramatically in the middle of the twentieth century.⁴ They were associated with important interest groups or social movements, which provided them with clients and money, and which interacted with them in developing the ideological positions shaping the legal positions the lawyers put forward. We can describe this as a thickening of the institutional basis for rights assertions.

Second, political parties, often with an eye to social movements, built commitments to rights into their platforms. Party leaders, or competitors for party leadership, argued that the party would benefit in the short or long run from adopting one or another position on rights issues. Rights have always been components of party platforms, and the changes in the twentieth century involved the precise content of rights and their association with specific parties, not any change in the general relationship between rights and parties.

Finally, and most important, the venues for asserting rights changed. Through the nineteenth century, rights were asserted primarily in legislation and political campaigns, and only secondarily in courts. Courts played a larger role by the beginning of the twentieth century, but seeking rights provision through legislation adopted by representatives or by referenda remained quite important, especially for the labor movement, whose efforts to secure the rights of labor often took the form of seeking to keep courts out of their hair. By the end of the twentieth century, it seemed to many almost incoherent to seek to assert rights in any venue other than the courts. Statutes creating new rights were important not because they expressed a social commitment to those rights but because the rights they created could be enforced in court.

Detailed historical accounts of how particular rights claims emerged and were vindicated or rejected reveal large variations in details, and seeking some universal "mechanism" that explains them all would be inconsistent with the historical enterprise. Even so, a broad-brush picture of the main features of the twentieth century rights revolution, one that connects in general terms the ideas and institutions that mattered for the revolution, begins with people who find themselves facing material conditions that they wish would be different. Some people put themselves forward as leaders of those people, and provide an account of how the material conditions could be changed. This account provides the glue that transforms the discontented into a social movement.[5] And, importantly, sometimes the movement's leaders articulate some right as an important part of their account of why things are bad and how they could be changed.[6]

If the social movement becomes large enough, politicians take notice. Some see the possibility of political advantage in seeking the movement's support. They appropriate, rearticulate, and transform the rights claim associated with the movement. If these political leaders are successful, the rights claim becomes part of a party platform, and, sometimes, part of the platforms of both major political parties. Legislative recognition of the rights claim may follow, although again we have to note the times at which and the ways in which the political versions of rights claims differ from the social movement's version. The right, no longer a claim, then can become embedded in executive and, sometimes, corporate bureaucracies, where lawyers take its enforcement as part of their duty to comply with the law.

Alternatively, the rights claim may be vindicated in courts. A political party that sees the social movement as an important constituent will ensure that the judges its leaders appoint or confirm are sympathetic to the rights claim. Or, particularly when leaders in both major parties offer support for the rights claim, judges already on the bench may begin to think that a rights claim that they previously had not thought valid actually has more force than they earlier believed.[7]

The story told here is about *successful* assertions of rights claims. A more complete account might expand our attention to the fact that rights assertions seem to come in waves, with some succeeding and others failing (at least for the moment). Each receding wave leaves its residue in ideas about rights and in institutions for asserting them, and sometimes those residues may have important effects later on. The reader should be aware of this phenomenon as this essay approaches the present. As the time between the events described and the present diminishes, the more uncertainty there is about what is a permanent achievement and what is going to be part of the residue as time passes.

# *Ideas*

*I*deas about rights are always complex when they are brought to ground in law. Elaborating the details of a particular right inevitably raises questions about the scope of the right, whether it should be limited by other rights, the extent to which general social policies can limit rights, and more. At one time one understanding of rights, and of specific rights, may prevail, and then be displaced in the legal culture by other ideas. The older ideas do not disappear, though. They hang on, sometimes serving as one basis for criticizing the new order and sometimes offering an alternative to which the nation might return. What follows attempts to identify the central tendencies of rights discourse through the twentieth century, but the reader should always remember that older ideas never disappear, and sometimes affect the way in which newer ones develop.[8]

## The Starting Point

Among lawyers at the end of the nineteenth century, the conceptual framework for addressing rights questions was reasonably well developed. Deploying that framework in particular cases was less stable, although some approaches clearly predominated over others. The instability in application provided the opening wedge for critiques that began early and became increasingly credible in the first decades of the twentieth century. Meanwhile, popular discourse about rights did not respect the lawyers' categories, but precisely because it was popular had less coherent conceptual underpinnings.

Lawyers sorted rights into three categories:

❖ Civil rights. These rights arose from the mere existence of organized society. Drawing on the social contract tradition, lawyers treated the right to physical security, the right to own property, and the right to enter into contracts (and some associated rights essential to protecting those basic rights, such as the right to sue in court and to present evidence in support of one's claims) as civil rights. The Civil Rights Act of 1866, which provided that "citizens, of every race and color, without regard to any previous condition of slavery or involuntary servitude ... shall have the same right, in every State and Territory in the United States, to make and enforce contracts, to sue, be parties, and give evidence, to inherit, purchase, lease, sell, hold, and convey real and personal property ... as is enjoyed by white citizens," used this idea of civil rights.

❖ Political rights. These arose from the political organization of particular societies. A society might not have jury trials, but if it did, the right to sit on juries was a political right—as of course was the right to vote.

❖ Social rights. In many ways this was a residual category, covering all the activities of daily life that did not implicate contract or property. As Rebecca Scott pointed out, the term *social equality* functioned in the late nineteenth century as a pejorative, identifying areas of life in which close associations between whites and other racial groups were regarded—by whites—as especially to be avoided.[9]

With important qualifications, governments could not deny anyone either civil or political rights, but had no duty to protect social rights.[10] They could limit social rights by exercising their traditional police powers, defined expansively to include not only promotion of safety and health, but public morals as well. Indeed, governments might be barred from seeking to advance social rights if protecting one person's social rights would limit another's civil rights.

Because they were baseline rights, civil and political rights had notions of equality built into them. For example, late nineteenth-century lawyers justified denying the right to vote to women by invoking their perceived lack of qualifications on the basic rights. These rights were available to everyone who satisfied requirements of capacity, defined in terms of the ability to deliberate and choose rationally, and independence, defined as a person's ability to come to conclusions without being unduly influenced by another who held economic power over the person. (These requirements were part of social contract theory, and of the common law of contracts and property as well. The constitutional law of capacity and independence did not track the common law rules precisely, though, which left room for some legislative interventions.) Women could be denied the right to vote on grounds of both capacity and dependence. To some, their more emotional responses to problems of public policy meant that they did not have the capacity to participate in making public policy; to others, the economic dependence of women on their fathers or husbands meant that they were subject to undue influence.

Ideas of equality played an additional role. Drawing on roots going back at least to the Jacksonian period, late nineteenth-century constitutional theory was hostile to what was described as "class legislation." Such legislation promoted the interests not of the people as a whole, but only the interests of a segment of the people. Discerning when a statute was merely class legislation was of course difficult. Opponents of a statute might call it class legislation, but its proponents ordinarily could deploy arguments aimed at demonstrating that the proposal advanced the general interest. Hostility to class legislation was therefore more a cast of mind that lawyers brought to their consideration of particular statutes than a doctrine uncontroversially invoked to explain why a statute was unconstitutional.[11]

Several important cases illustrate these categories.

❖ *Plessy v. Ferguson* (1896) upheld a state law requiring that railroads maintain separate cars for white and African American travelers. According to the Supreme Court, the right to ride in a particular car was merely a social right.[12]

❖ *Holden v. Hardy* (1898) upheld a state law limiting the time miners could work to eight hours a day. Mining was risky and unhealthy, and the government could use its police powers to protect miners. In addition, according to the Court, there was reason to think that miners were not sufficiently independent to have a civil right to sign contracts requiring that they work long hours: "the proprietors lay down the rules and the laborers are practically constrained to obey them. In such cases, self-interest is often an unsafe guide, and the legislature may properly interpose its authority."[13]

❖ *Lochner v. New York* (1905) struck down a state law limiting bakers to ten working hours a day. The Supreme Court found insufficient evidence that limiting working hours made it more likely that bakery products would be safe for consumers, or less likely that bakery workers would be healthy. And there was no reason to think that bakers were less able than any other workers to make good decisions about their own interests—that is, no reason to think that bakery workers either lacked capacity to contract or were too dependent on others.[14]

❖ *Muller v. Oregon* (1908) upheld a state law limiting to eight the hours women could work in laundries. The Court's decision invoked both the police power—the ability of the state to intervene in a contractual relation because of women's distinctive physical capacity—and women's dependence on men: "history discloses the fact that woman has always been dependent upon man. ... Though limitations upon personal and contractual rights may be removed by legislation, there is that in her disposition and habits of life which will operate against a full assertion of those rights. ... It is impossible to close one's eyes to the fact that she still looks to her brother, and depends upon him. ... The two sexes differ in ... the self-reliance which enables one to assert full rights."[15]

❖ *Buchanan v. Warley* (1917) invalidated a Louisville ordinance requiring residential segregation. The ordinance prohibited African Americans from buying houses on blocks where whites were a majority and whites from buying houses on blocks with African American majorities. The Court's opinion emphasized that the ordinance interfered with the owner's ordinary right to sell his property at the price he chose to the person he chose.[16]

❖ *Meyer v. Nebraska* (1923) struck down a state law prohibiting instruction in German, even in private schools. The Court offered two reasons for its decision. The first fit easily into the existing conceptual framework: the statute "attempted materially to interfere with the calling of modern language teachers," and thereby deprived them of their right to enter into contracts with parents who wanted their children educated in German. The second was broader, more compatible with modern liberalism's emphasis on personal autonomy, here the autonomy of parents from the state: the Constitution protected "the right of the individual to contract, to engage in any of the common occupations of life, to acquire useful knowledge, to marry, establish a home and bring up children, to worship God according to the dictates of his own conscience, and generally to enjoy those privileges long recognized at common law as essential to the orderly pursuit of happiness by free men."[17]

Many of these cases have an undoubted libertarian flavor, but classical liberalism was not modern libertarianism or mere laissez faire. When private contracts had effects on third parties—people who were not part of the contractual relationship—the Court upheld a wide range of regulatory statutes as valid exercises of the government's police powers, even when those regulations might have been characterized as interfering with someone's right to property or contract. No one seriously questioned the constitutionality of provisions in New York's law regulating bakeries that prohibited workers from sleeping at their workplace, for example. The reason is that such a practice might well render the workplace unsanitary, and so affect the quality and safety of the bread the workers made. *Plessy* provides another example: railroads and African Americans might have been happy to make contracts allowing the latter to ride on any car they wished, but, as the legislature and the Court saw things, those contracts affected the social rights of whites who wanted to ride in segregated cars. The contracts between the railroads and African Americans could therefore be regulated.

The Court consistently rejected statutes it regarded, in a phrase used in *Lochner*, as a "labor law as such"—that is, as legislation resting on the assumption that ordinary workers could not bargain effectively with their employers. Nor did the Court write the common law's definitions of capacity and dependence into the Constitution. No one thought that courts could refuse to enforce miners' agreements to work long hours in states without a maximum hours law—that is, that miners lacked capacity under the common law. Rather, the Court recognized some power in the legislature to alter traditional common-law definitions, at least to some extent.[18]

Most of the constitutional issues at the heart of late nineteenth-century discourse were bound up with economic regulation, and not with the issues of free expression and equality that came to dominate rights discourse in the twentieth century. But the libertarian tendencies associated with the earlier discourse had implications for those issues as well. As political scientist Mark Graber and legal scholar David Rabban have shown, while courts were unsympathetic to free speech claims during this period, a vigorous libertarian jurisprudence of free expression developed, and was available when political liberals began to worry about government regulation of speech.[19] And, to the extent that Jim Crow was a system of legal regulation that extended into the domain of social rights, *Buchanan v. Warley* showed how libertarian tendencies could support claims for racial equality.[20]

The discourse of civil, political, and social rights was a *lawyer's* discourse. Ordinary citizens, and particularly those associated with the late nineteenth-century labor movement, talked of rights more diffusely. For them, the rights of labor were whatever seemed necessary or appropriate to ensure that workers were able to lead decent lives. The voluntarist elements in the labor movement were actively hostile to judicial enforcement of rights, because they believed that the courts would inevitably side with employers. William Forbath described voluntarism as teaching "that workers should pursue improvements in their living conditions through collective bargaining and concerted action in the private sphere rather than through public political action."[21] As Samuel Gompers put it, the "best thing the State can do for Labor is to leave Labor alone."[22]

Gompers had reason for his belief. Voluntarists were willing to bargain with employers to obtain maximum hours, desirable conditions of work, and, of course, guaranteed wages. To get employers to the bargaining table and then to agree to terms, though, workers had to be able to use economic force by withholding their labor and discouraging others from taking their place. Courts in the late nineteenth and early twentieth centuries regularly applied common-law doctrines about interference with contractual relations to restrict unions' ability to conduct effective strikes.[23] Put another way, the rights courts enforced were employers' rights, not the rights of labor. Better, to the voluntarists, for the courts to step aside—and, if abandoning the idea of rights was necessary to that end, so be it. The craft unions that were Gompers's main constituency believed their economic power vis-à-vis their employers was great enough to allow them to accomplish more than courts were willing to see done by legislation.

Voluntarists were not entirely comfortable with securing the rights of labor through legislation either. In part that flowed from the idea of voluntarism itself. In addition, the lawyers' conceptual categories pushed in the direction of defending labor legislation by asserting that some workers, at least, did not have the capacity to contract—an assertion that no labor leader could afford to make with respect to workers generally.

Other supporters of the labor movement, though, believed that the rights of labor could be secured through legislation. They had no need to develop careful conceptual categories to sort out what the rights of labor were, or how they related to the rights already recognized and described by the lawyers' categories. That would be a task for the future. For the present, what was needed was legislative recognition of the rights of labor, whether those rights were protection against judicial interference with collective bargaining or substantive guarantees of good working conditions and the like. Workers then could enforce the rights of labor directly by pressure on employers in negotiations or through public criticism.

Yet, the lawyers' conceptual categories, while widely used, were not self-defining. In nearly every case the categories themselves could have been developed to reach the result the Court rejected. *Plessy*, for example, could easily have been characterized as a case in which the legislature infringed on the railroads' civil right to offer whatever contracts they thought would provide them the most profit. Some undoubtedly would offer only segregated cars, but others might offer both segregated and unsegregated cars, perhaps charging different fares. Price discrimination, not race discrimination, would accommodate everyone's social rights. The market, not the government, would decide which outcome was socially desirable. Similarly, the notion of limited capacity used in *Holden* was available in *Lochner*. In the former, the Court assumed that people who worked in mines had to accept the terms offered them by mine-owners. Why people who worked in bakeries were different is unclear. (The Court seems to have assumed that bakers faced with unattractive terms could simply walk away and take some other employment, but that seems true of miners as well. It is not obvious that miners' alternative employment opportunities were more limited than bakers'.)

Maximum hours laws (and their counterpart, minimum wage laws) were an important part of the political agenda of organized labor and its Progressive allies. In addition, *Lochner*'s doctrine placed a great deal of Progressive legislation under a cloud. The courts might eventually uphold regulatory legislation, but it would take time and additional effort to defend the legislation. These concerns fueled the effort to develop a critique of the way in which rights protection was conceptualized at the turn of the twentieth century.

## Pragmatic and Realist Critiques

Political progressives in the early years of the twentieth century were pragmatists philosophically, not in any formal sense, but in the sense that a rough pragmatic approach was the working philosophy of political progressivism. The pragmatic philosophers, led by John Dewey, developed a jurisprudence, sometimes described as sociological jurisprudence, that placed the idea of rights under real pressure. To pragmatists, social policy—and constitutional law—rested in the end on a careful balancing of interests.[24] Yet, the very point of identifying something as a constitutional right was to block consideration of some social interests. Pragmatism weakened the distinction between rights and mere social policy, at a time when legal pragmatists were insisting that courts had given inadequate attention to social policy by erecting strong and pragmatically indefensible barriers to legislation in the name of rights.

*Meyer v. Nebraska* provides a good example. Justice James McReynolds's opinion conceded that the nation had an interest in ensuring that its people understood "American ideals" and would be "prepared to understand current discussions of civic matters." For legal pragmatists, the real question was whether restricting instruction to English would assist in promoting that interest. But *Meyer* said nothing about that question. At the point where a legal pragmatist would have taken it up, Justice McReynolds asserted in conclusory terms, "Perhaps it would be highly advantageous if all had ready understanding of our ordinary speech, but this cannot be coerced by methods which conflict with the Constitution—a desirable end cannot be promoted by prohibited means."

Legal pragmatists might have treated *Buchanan v. Warley* similarly. Justice William Day's opinion acknowledged that maintaining segregated neighborhoods might promote social peace and avoid violence between the races. The civil rights to property and contract blocked the Court from making the serious sociological inquiry into that possibility that legal pragmatism recommended.

From the perspective of the late twentieth century, the legal pragmatists' approach to free speech may be more interesting. Governments at every level tried hard during World War I to regulate speech because they feared its dissemination would interfere with the war effort. Advocates of free speech rights insisted that remote consequences of speech, such as the possibility that some listener might conclude from the speech that some illegal action to interfere with the war effort was desirable, should be ignored, and only proximate effects considered. For the pragmatists, that was a mistake. Constitutional law might discount remote effects but it could not ignore them completely.

John Dewey wrote several essays for the progressive journal *The New Republic* on rights during wartime. He saw the war as a chance to displace "the individualistic tradition" of the United States and assert "the supremacy of public need over private possessions." Dewey's own judgments on free speech were temperately supportive of wartime dissenters, although as legal historian David Rabban observed, he did not "express any concern for the dissenters themselves" and criticized them for an individualism that he associated with the idea of rights. Harvard Law School dean Roscoe Pound was even more skeptical about dissenters' claims that their rights were being violated. Law, even constitutional law, involved a balancing of interests, and rights-claims were simply one among many interests. His published writings were even more moderately in support of dissent in wartime, although in a private letter he observed that "in time of insurrection, riot, or war the general interest in public security may require us to put the lid on for the time being."[25]

Legal pragmatists focused more on the interests of labor than on other rights, and there their critique of rights had more bite. They disdained the rhetoric of "the rights of labor," turning their attention to the fact that the rights courts were enforcing against labor were employers' rights. Legal pragmatists were more sympathetic than the *Lochner* Court to empirical evidence showing that police power regulations served social purposes. But, even more, they contended that there was nothing wrong with a labor law "as such." There were, legal pragmatists believed, social interests in ensuring that workers were well off enough—an interest in preserving social peace if material conditions were truly desperate, and an interest in promoting collective bargaining on more equal terms once some basic needs were secured. The rights of labor could be secured only by affirmative government action.[26]

The pragmatists' sociological jurisprudence of competing interests left little room for constitutional rights. As historian Eric Foner put it, "'Freedom' was not the most prominent word in the vocabulary of Progressivism."[27] Pragmatists could accept a practice in which the result of the consideration of all the relevant interests got the label "right," as long as the label did not lead people to believe that concepts given that label had some force beyond the balance of considerations already built into particular rights. But, wary of the possibility that labels misled, legal pragmatists were generally unsympathetic to the rhetoric of rights.

World War I saw a concerted assault on what we now think of as free speech rights. Liberals and Progressives were divided over the merits of the free speech claims made by political radicals and opponents of the war. In part, that was because American participation in the war was the project of President Woodrow Wilson, himself a Progressive, who depicted the war as one whose goal was the extension of democracy. And in part it was because the rights claims were made by radicals with whom liberals and Progressives were at odds in politics. But also it was because liberals and Progressives had developed a jurisprudence in which rights were associated with conservatism and the status quo, and in which the rights people had were the result of a careful balancing of competing social interests. In Foner's words, "Civil liberties, by and large, had never been a major concern of Progressivism, which had always viewed the national state as the embodiment of democratic purpose and insisted that freedom flowed from participating in the life of society, not standing in isolated opposition."[28]

The discomfort with the idea of rights associated with pragmatism and sociological jurisprudence found expression in the characteristic form of Progressive-era legislation. Instead of enacting statutes creating rights enforced in courts, Progressives created agencies to administer workers' compensation laws and gave experts a central role in administering new systems of juvenile justice. Progressives looked to experts and new institutional forms because they believed that the conceptual categories lawyers and courts used were inconsistent with the more nuanced set of values that good public policy—and therefore good constitutional law—required.

Progressive discomfort with the courts found its way into constitutional theory as well. Progressives spent a great deal of political energy defending labor's legislative victories against constitutional challenge. Picking up a theme extending far back into U.S. constitutional history, they worried about the relative roles of courts and legislatures in assessing when legislation violated the Constitution. Pragmatism required the consideration of many facts about the world, and the balancing of competing social interests. Pragmatists questioned whether courts were better at assessing those facts and balancing those interests than legislatures. Writing in *The New Republic*, law professor Felix Frankfurter regularly invoked institutional considerations in his criticisms of the Supreme Court's use of the due process clause to invalidate progressive legislation.[29]

Representing the defenders of the maximum hours law for women workers in *Muller*, Louis Brandeis pioneered in the presentation of evidence about social conditions—precisely the kind of evidence sociological jurisprudence thought central to the development of good social policy. The Court was not quite sure how to treat Brandeis's brief. Justice David Brewer referred to the evidence Brandeis assembled, saying that they were "not ... technically speaking authorities," and insisting that "[c]onstitutional questions ... are not settled by even a consensus of current public opinion," but concluded that "widespread belief" should be considered "when a question of fact is debated and debatable."[30]

Technical expertise and empirical examinations of social reality were not the only contributions that university-affiliated pragmatists made to constitutional theory in the early decades of the twentieth century. Insights drawn from the nascent field of political science cast doubt on classical liberalism's hostility to class legislation. Arthur Bentley described class legislation as the ordinary product of groups operating in the legislative process.[31] Stripped of some of Bentley's quasi-philosophical excesses, an interest-group approach to legislation helped Progressives explain why laws that seemed to benefit only part of society should be regarded as standard and obviously constitutional. Eventually, interest-group influences on legislation expanded and became, once again, a source of concern. When that happened, a further transformation of constitutional thinking occurred as well.

Exemplary of sociological jurisprudence, the Brandeis brief highlights an asymmetry in legal pragmatism bolstered by institutional analysis: it was well suited for upholding contested legislation, not so well suited for explaining why legislative determinations about complex facts—such as facts about the causal connection between speech and illegal activity, or between racial proximity and violence—should be overturned. That asymmetry did not matter when Progressives were defending their legislative accomplishments against attack. It came to matter when Progressivism expanded, in the aftermath of World War I, to include concern for racial equality and free speech.

The pragmatic commitment to balancing fit well with the ideas associated with the social gospel, and later with the social teachings of the Catholic Church—the former initially associated with Progressives mostly in the Republican party, the latter associated with Democrats and their immigrant-based urban political machines, and brought to the New Deal by Monsignor John A. Ryan. Notably, though, the policies advanced by the social gospel and the church's social teachings were plainly unsuited for judicial enforcement. Even more, ideas like the "common good," central to the social teachings, and parallel ideas within the social gospel, could not easily be translated into the language of rights.[32]

Some in the pragmatic tradition took the critique even deeper. Some legal realists worked with the lawyers' categories of civil, political, and social rights, to the end of demonstrating that the categories had *no* determinate content. *Plessy* could have been a case about the civil right to contract, *Lochner* a case about the legislature's power to expand the concept of capacity to contract beyond its common law boundaries. And, on the other side, *Buchanan* could have been reconstructed as a case about the social right to select those with whom one would associate: those who wished to exercise their social right to live far away from African Americans found that right undermined by a few people—about to leave the neighborhood anyway—who were willing to sell houses to African Americans. They solved what we would today call a collective action problem by securing legislation to prevent others from interfering with their social rights.[33]

Legal realists found the lawyers' traditional categories empty. Much in the realists' arguments about constitutional law arose first in their critiques of the common law. According to the realists, courts applying the common law purported to invoke seemingly obvious propositions, such as that courts should not interfere with the agreements people made. But, the realists pointed out, common-law judges did not in fact endorse those propositions. They qualified them: courts should indeed interfere with contracts predicated on fraud, or where one party was so deficient that the contract could not fairly be attributed to his own choice. These qualifications undermined the claim that courts applying the common law were simply enforcing neutral and nonpolitical criteria.

The realist critique could extend to constitutional law. The qualifications found within the common law were relevant as well to the standard conceptual categories, and particularly to the idea of civil rights. So, for example, that category could make sense of unquestionable legal rules such as the denial of rights to children and the insane only by including a qualification that civil rights could be held only by those with the capacity to make contracts and own property. Defenders of the traditional categories then had to spell out exactly what constituted that capacity. In doing so, they imported criteria such as rationality and independence from their common law counterparts. The realists then pushed their criticisms of the common law into new terrain. And, importantly, defenders of the traditional categories did not have the resources—within the law itself—to resist that development. All they could do was assert what all came to see were merely political objections, not conceptual ones.

Alternatively, legal realists showed how particular problems posed conflicts between rights. Sometimes the conflicts were between rights in the same category. One person's civil right to own property conflicted with another person's right to enter into contracts. The aftermath of *Buchanan v. Warley* provides an example. Deprived of the ability to secure legislation guaranteeing racially segregated neighborhoods, property owners wrote restrictions on the power to sell one's property, known as racially restrictive covenants, into their deeds. Restrictive covenants presented problems within property theory, but also within constitutional law: property law allowed some contractual provisions—some restrictive covenants—to qualify the ordinary property right to sell to whoever one chose, but not all conceivable restrictive covenants. Into which class did the racially restrictive covenant fall? Legal realists argued that legal analysis, on its own, could not provide an answer. (The Supreme Court avoided the question by asserting in 1926 that the mere presence of racially restrictive covenants in property deeds did not implicate the Constitution at all. Twenty years later it said that the state's enforcement of such covenants did violate the Constitution.)[34]

Sometimes the conflicts were between categories, as in *Plessy* where the railroads' right to contract conflicted with white customers' social right of association. The legal realist critique, on the first level, simply demanded that the courts *address* the existence of a conflict, something entirely absent in *Plessy*. But, what were courts to do once they noticed a conflict? Ranking rights—treating social rights as more important than civil rights, or vice versa—was not a promising strategy, because the categories contained widely diverse particular rights, and the grounds for ranking were quite unclear. Instead, the realists insisted that all the courts could do was choose which right to treat as more important in the circumstances.

The legal realist approach to rights provided some leverage on the institutional concerns Frankfurter articulated. Because the legal concepts used to analyze rights claims had no content at all, everyone called upon to participate in the processes of constitutionalism simply had to make choices that were not legal but political or ideological. At least as long as judicial review existed, judges could only choose—and they were at no disadvantage relative to legislatures with respect to choice alone. The legal realist analysis did not significantly diverge from sociological jurisprudence while progressives were out of power, but it came to have real bite once the Supreme Court's composition shifted to favor progressivism.

## The New Deal Reconstruction

Once Progressives gained firm control of the Supreme Court in the late 1930s, they had to make a strategic choice, described by political scientist Martin Shapiro as a choice between dismantling the weapons the Supreme Court had developed and which their opponents had used against them, or turning those weapons against their opponents.[35] The debate over that choice persisted through mid-century, with the advocates of dismantling the weapons—that is, a systematic pursuit of judicial restraint—gradually losing ground to those who sought to reconstruct a jurisprudence based on individual rights that was somehow stripped of the libertarian leanings of classical liberalism.

The choice was closely connected to the construction of the New Deal Democratic coalition. On the level of ideas, the pragmatists' attraction to replacing the language of rights with the language of social interests served well to defend the New Deal's major initiatives, such as the creation of the Social Security system and the general regulatory thrust of New Deal interventions in the economy. Indeed, in selecting nominees for the Supreme Court, Franklin Roosevelt paid attention only to whether they would uphold these initiatives. Inevitably, then, pragmatic balancing and suspicion of rights-based claims would have a foothold on the Supreme Court.

Pragmatism, though, provided few resources in the areas of modern civil liberties such as freedom of speech and racial equality. Notably, by the mid-1930s the categories of classical constitutional theory had disappeared completely from constitutional discourse. The term "civil rights" now referred to the constitutional interest in securing racial equality, the term "political rights" had been replaced by "civil liberties," and the idea that there were social rights had no more than a residual influence in political rhetoric. Pragmatic balancing was unsuited to determining whether civil rights and civil liberties were at risk, because it gave no special analytic status to those interests.

The key move made in the judicial theory of constitutional rights in the 1930s had two components: a sharp differentiation between the economic interests at the heart of the New Deal and civil liberties and civil rights, which were at most of collateral and long-term interest to New Dealers, accompanied by a justification for that differentiation that brought the earlier institutional concerns about judicial capacity to the fore. Justice Harlan Fiske Stone provided the classic formulation of this move in a case that would otherwise have remained obscure, a constitutional challenge rooted in classical liberalism to a New Deal regulation prohibiting the sale of "filled milk," a cheap and nutritious substitute for whole milk. The New Deal Court had little difficulty upholding the statute (*United States v. Carolene Products*, 1938).[36] The case became famous because of its "Footnote 4." Attached to a sentence saying that courts would defer to legislative judgments on matters of economic regulation, Footnote 4 asserted that there might be room for more aggressive judicial intervention when litigants claimed either that a statute violated a specific prohibition in the Bill of Rights or, more important for the development of the modern liberal idea of rights, if they claimed that legislation interfered with or resulted from defects in the democratic process, with prejudice against "discrete and insular minorities" counting as such a defect.

Obvious on the surface of Footnote 4 jurisprudence was a new concern for the constitutional rights of African Americans, and a concern for freedom of expression derived from liberals' reflections on the experience of World War I and its aftermath (and on the effects of attacks on the free speech rights of labor organizers and political radicals, who were at least for the moment the allies of the New Deal). But the implications of that jurisprudence were far more extensive.

The liberalism associated with the New Deal defended deference to legislative judgments with respect to economic regulation on institutional grounds. According to the emerging theory of constitutional rights, economic regulation raised complex questions of fact and value. Legislatures had better resources to determine facts than did courts. More important, legislative judgments of value reflected the values held by legislators' constituents. The pragmatic critique of classical liberal constitutional law established, to the satisfaction of mid-century liberals, that value judgments about economic regulation were "essentially contested." (That term was appropriated in the 1960s from its use in a major article about moral and political philosophy, but the concept was roughly available to New Deal jurisprudence earlier.) New Deal liberalism contended that in an area where value disagreement was inevitable, courts should defer to the decisions of representative legislatures because whatever might be said on the merits of the value judgments, those decisions had a warrant in the theory of majority rule that judicial value choices lacked, or at least had in much weaker form.

All well and good, for the matters New Dealers were most concerned about. There was another theme in New Deal and legal realist jurisprudence, with implications for the new civil rights and civil liberties. The legal realist critique of libertarian-leaning protections of property and contract was that those categories gained content only through substantive analysis, which had to take into account the distribution of power between employers and workers. Overruling earlier decisions invalidating minimum wage and maximum hours laws, Chief Justice Charles Evans Hughes suggested that the government had an affirmative duty to protect "liberty" against "the evils which menace the health, safety, morals, and welfare of the people." Employers who paid less than the minimum wage were "in effect" receiving "a subsidy" from the public that was called upon to support the needy.[37] This perspective linked constitutional law to background rules of property law, with the former responding to inadequacies of the latter. Chief Justice Hughes probably did not understand that his approach thrust constitutional rights into every space in society, and forced courts to determine the merits of every constitutional claim without the deference to the legislature to which New Dealers were also committed.

Footnote 4 jurisprudence, though, brought that implication to the fore. That jurisprudence argued that courts could identify situations in which legislation lacked the democratic warrant that New Dealers relied on to explain judicial deference on economic regulation. Here the emerging theory of constitutional rights could also draw on the sharper-edged legal realist critiques of economic rights as well. Generalized to all rights, those critiques suggested that there were no "democratic institutions" independent of the courts' determination that a particular institution was indeed democratic. The point was obvious in cases like *Colegrove v. Green* (1946), a challenge to the malapportionment of the Illinois congressional delegation.[38] Justice Frankfurter argued that the courts should stay out of apportionment controversies because they could be resolved only if one adopted a substantive theory of democratic representation, the kind of value judgment that courts were unsuited to provide. But, although the Court refused to intervene in *Colegrove*, Frankfurter's colleagues understood that his argument did not fit the issue before them: he was asking them to defer to the judgments of Illinois's legislature because those judgments had a warrant in democratic representation that a court's judgment would lack, but did so in a context where the claim was precisely that the legislative judgment could not be defended by referring to the legislature's democratic credentials.[39]

Footnote 4 jurisprudence played another role: it allowed the courts to maintain their place as important institutions of governance in a post-New Deal world where they had withdrawn from supervision of the legislature's efforts to regulate the economy. Justice Frankfurter's assertion of a generalized posture of deference to legislative judgment would have relegated the courts to the margins of the governing process, and when given the choice political actors rarely consign themselves to supporting roles. Notably, even Justice Frankfurter could not sustain his theoretical position in practice; he supported a rather interventionist judicial role in enforcing the anti-establishment principle in church-state law, and was quite aggressive in placing limits on police searches.

From the New Deal through the early 1960s, the jurisprudence of Footnote 4 explained nearly everything the Supreme Court did, as law professor John Hart Ely showed in one of the leading works of constitutional theory in the late twentieth century (*Democracy and Distrust*, 1980). The Court refrained from striking down economic regulations, but developed an elaborate law of free expression and racial equality. Ely showed that judicial practice and constitutional theory had accepted the jurisprudence of Footnote 4, even when particular results were controversial.

Even decisions enforcing rights in the criminal process fit, albeit imperfectly, into a Footnote 4 mold because they were at least in important measure often about the ramifications of race in criminal law enforcement. The Scottsboro cases, involving the convictions of several African Americans of rape and an ensuing large-scale publicity campaign attacking the convictions, generated two important constitutional decisions. *Powell v. Alabama* (1932) held that the defendants had been denied due process of law because the state had severely truncated their ability to get decent legal representation at their trials. The decision generated others, culminating in the Warren Court's decision thirty years later in *Gideon v. Wainwright* (1963) that all defendants facing significant prison sentences were entitled to legal representation, at the state's expense if necessary. *Norris v. Alabama* (1935) applied long-standing rules to overturn a second round of convictions in the Scottsboro cases, holding that African Americans had unconstitutionally been excluded from the juries.[40] Justice Hugo Black, whose appointment to the Supreme Court was tainted by his postconfirmation acknowledgement that he had been a member of the racist Ku Klux Klan, wrote the Court's opinion overturning the conviction of an African American defendant whose confession had been beaten out of him, saying that, in contrast to totalitarian nations like Germany and Soviet Russia, in the United States "courts stand against any winds that blow as havens of refuge for those who might otherwise suffer because they are helpless, weak, outnumbered, or because they are nonconforming victims of prejudice and public excitement" (*Chambers v. Florida*, 1939).[41] The more comprehensive interventions in the criminal justice system by the Warren Court in the 1960s rarely addressed questions of race specifically, but it is clear that they were motivated by concern that many urban police forces and prosecutors actively constructed a racist system of criminal justice.

Footnote 4 jurisprudence would run into trouble near the end of the twentieth century, when the simple New Deal vision of how democracy worked came under pressure from political scientists, who emphasized the way in which interest groups could disconnect legislative value judgments from the judgments held by legislators' constituents, and from economists working in the field of "public choice," who developed more formal models explaining why that disconnect occurred.[42] Interest-group accounts of the legislative process generated a proliferation of "discrete and insular minorities." Any interest group could be so characterized, at least with the exercise of a bit of ingenuity. The proliferation of such "minorities" opened up two possibilities. One could follow Footnote 4 faithfully, and allow judicial intervention in every case that an analyst could describe as the result of an interest-group deal in which some discrete and insular minority—typically, the consumer or general interest—was disregarded. Or one could urge the courts to abstain from intervention in all cases, arguing that discrete and insular minorities might have lost on a particular question, but certainly were in a position to bargain and win on other issues. By the 1960s, for example, the political power of African Americans, the group for whom the category "discrete and insular minority" had been invented, was large enough to make questionable the use of Footnote 4 jurisprudence as a basis for striking down laws on the ground that they discriminated against African Americans—unless, of course, one used a fancy enough Footnote 4 theory, with all sorts of implications for the theory's general scope.

Other modes of analysis were coming to displace Footnote 4, though, and these difficulties remained largely theoretical. For the most part, criticisms of the legislative process as excessively influenced by narrow interest groups undermined the case for judicial deference to legislative judgments about economic regulation—that is, about the text to which Footnote 4 was attached—and, if anything, provided even greater support for the judicial interventions suggested by the footnote itself.

Footnote 4 jurisprudence, resting as it did on an account of the relative capacities and incapacities of courts and legislatures, could not coherently be a jurisprudence for rights discussions by politicians and their constituents. Unavailable within the discourse of Footnote 4 jurisprudence, appeals to economic rights continued in politics. The New Deal's commitment to ensuring the possibility of collective bargaining was regularly described as "Labor's Bill of Rights," for example, and once again in a context where the entire point of securing the rights was to get away from the courts and their intrusions on bargaining between labor and management. The New Deal embedded government social provision into the world of statutory rights. The Social Security Act, national unemployment compensation legislation, and eventually a general system of public assistance to the poor were statutory "entitlements," that is, rights. Often limited in scope by racism and sexism—federal minimum wage laws excluded agricultural workers from coverage, for example, because too many such workers were African Americans—these statutory rights nonetheless became an important component of the rights revolution.

Franklin Roosevelt's State of the Union address in 1944 urged that the nation should adopt a "Second Bill of Rights," which would guarantee jobs with decent wages, medical care, homeownership, and more.[43] These were offered as rights for legislative implementation. Congress responded with the feeble Employment Act of 1946, which watered down the jobs guarantee, and then killed President Harry Truman's proposal for universal medical care. The language of rights continued to have some hold on the public imagination in legislative settings, but that hold was clearly weaker than the idea of rights as objects of special judicial attention. That the Second Bill of Rights would have been a social democratic document, guaranteeing what came to be called second-generation rights, of course mattered too for its enervation, in light of the weakness of the social democratic tradition in the United States. Late in the century, some aspects of social provision came under attack, under the name of "entitlement reform." The very term, though, suggests that rights ideas still mattered. And, though some entitlement reforms did occur, they ran up against a wall when the reforms threatened to eliminate entirely the safety nets for the poor, and to threaten income support for the elderly. With some reason, we can say that as a practical matter the United States did recognize these statutory provisions as rights guarantees.

## The Emergence of Modern Liberalism: Autonomy and Accommodation

The transformation of liberal rights discourse in the New Deal persisted through the end of the twentieth century. But, in the last third of the century, modern liberalism took on a new cast. In addition to guarantees of rights associated with democracy, modern liberalism reintroduced libertarian themes, not as in the first instance in connection with economics, but rather with respect to personal autonomy. Concern for personal autonomy generated support for rights not previously recognized within New Deal jurisprudence—a development that some liberals such as Ely found both baffling and unprincipled—but also injected new elements into previously recognized rights. Developments in constitutional law and in legislation led constitutional law to incorporate the idea that, sometimes, equality could be achieved in markets and through legislative mandates only if those subject to regulation were required not only to refrain from discriminating against certain groups but were required as well to accommodate those groups. These developments were sufficiently widespread—arising in connection with the extended process of desegregation, with affirmative action, with pregnancy discrimination, with discrimination against persons with disabilities—as to provoke a broader rethinking of what equality required. By the end of the century, the idea that equality was a matter of substance and not only of form had become embedded in American constitutionalism. Embedded, but not firmly implanted, because substantive equality inevitably pushes in the direction of recognizing entitlements to social democratic rights.

At the same time, classical liberalism staged a comeback, but in a new form. The libertarian strand of classical liberalism resurfaced as a concern that legislatures oppressed minorities. In the economic domain oppression took the form of regulations that prevented ambitious entrepreneurs from starting their own small businesses. Elsewhere oppression took the form of affirmative action programs that were said to disadvantage white members of immigrant groups who came to the United States after slavery had been abolished. Even those in the new Christian Right who sought to infuse public policy with specifically religious content framed some of their claims in terms of rights to equal participation in the democratic process, and not as justifiable efforts to create a nation committed to religious belief.

Autonomy became an important component of modern liberalism for several reasons. Prodded by law professor Ronald Dworkin and philosopher John Rawls, legal theorists came to believe that their theorizing required some grounding in political theory, if only in rudimentary form. Political philosophers reminded them that classical liberalism and the democratic commitments arising from it rested, in the end, on the idea of individual autonomy. Modern liberals responded by adding a direct recognition of autonomy to the indirect recognition of autonomy expressed in their commitment to democracy, thereby creating the possibility of a clash between the direct protection of autonomy and intrusions on autonomy licensed by democratic decision-making. Modern liberals resolved the conflict in two ways. They denied democratic legitimacy to decisions by legislatures that failed Footnote 4's requirements; this dissolved the conflict. Creative reconstructions of Footnote 4 could go a long way here, but such reconstructions raised their own problems. In addition, when push came to shove, modern liberals insisted that the direct protection of personal autonomy prevail over the expressions even of well-functioning democratic legislatures.

World War II and the Cold War supported the development of direct protection of personal autonomy as well.[44] It seemed feeble to identify the problem with totalitarianism simply with the absence of democracy in Nazi Germany and the Soviet Union. George Orwell's image of a boot stamping on a human face forever, and of Winston Smith's "agreement"

     New Essays on American Constitutional History

after enhanced interrogation that two plus two might indeed equal five, were more potent and accurate in capturing totalitarianism's vices than the observation that totalitarian regimes were undemocratic: they were images of intrusions on human autonomy, and only remotely images of democratic failure. Scholarly studies of totalitarianism suggested as well that totalitarian governments could elicit simulacra of consent, like Winston Smith's, from their populations. Coupled with studies of advertising in the late 1940s and 1950s, this raised worries about the possibility that what appeared to be consent-based support for nominally democratic governments and their policies might be similarly ill founded. Only direct protection of personal autonomy could guard against that possibility.

The Supreme Court's criminal procedure decisions supported the emergence of autonomy as a theme in constitutional law as well. Although rather clearly motivated by concerns about race and justice, the decisions took the form of interpreting the Constitution's guarantees of fairness in criminal procedure in terms most directly understood as protections for personal autonomy. Searches intruded on domains of personal privacy, for example, and techniques of obtaining confessions might involve physical or psychological pressures that seemed to impair a person's will.

The proximate source of modern liberalism's concern for personal autonomy was the mid-century sexual revolution. Constitutional law first became concerned with government restrictions on sexual activity in challenges to laws prohibiting marriages across racial lines, which could have been addressed merely as problems of race discrimination. After avoiding decision on those questions to avoid heightening existing tensions over desegregation, the Supreme Court ultimately held such restrictions unconstitutionally discriminatory in 1964 and, definitively, in 1967 (*McLaughlin v. Florida*, 1964; *Loving v. Virginia*, 1967).[45] When personal autonomy emerged as a theme in modern liberalism, these cases were reconstructed as cases about the fundamental importance of one's ability to choose a marriage partner.

Meanwhile, *Griswold v. Connecticut* (1965) marked autonomy's arrival in constitutional law. There the Supreme Court held unconstitutional a Connecticut statute, one of only two in the country, that made it a crime to provide contraceptives even to married couples. The statute was never enforced, but for decades it had deterred family planning advocates from opening clinics that would supply contraceptives to their clients. Justice William O. Douglas's opinion for the Court purported to avoid reviving notions of substantive due process by drawing on a range of decided cases that showed that the Court had girded specific constitutional rights with "penumbras" that were essential to ensure that people could effectively exercise the enumerated rights. Other opinions in the case referred to the Ninth Amendment's recognition that the people retained rights not listed in the Bill of Rights. *Griswold* described the right it protected as a right to privacy, but it rapidly became clear that the right at issue was better described as a right to personal autonomy in making important decisions related mostly to sexual conduct—a right, that is, to insulate one's own decisions from regulation by the government.[46]

Within a decade *Griswold* became the basis in precedent for the Court's controversial decisions sharply restricting the ability of governments to regulate a woman's decision (in consultation with her doctor) to carry a pregnancy to term or to have an abortion. And just after the twenty-first century began the Court extended these precedents to invalidate state laws making consensual sexual contact between persons of the same sex unlawful (*Lawrence v. Texas*, 2003).[47] What is striking is how deeply embedded the constitutional protection of personal autonomy rapidly became. The legal theory supporting *Griswold* was controversial among scholars committed to the New Deal paradigm of constitutional law, but *Griswold*'s holding soon came to seem obviously correct to the public. Judge Robert Bork's nomination to the Supreme Court foundered on his principled position that he could find no basis in the Constitution for a free-standing right to privacy, which his opponents effectively presented to the public as a criticism of *Griswold*'s outcome. Thereafter nominees who disagreed with the Court's abortion decisions were careful to say that they did not challenge that holding, although they rarely presented an account of how they would justify overturning the abortion decisions without casting doubt on *Griswold* as well. Similarly, critics of the 2003 gay rights decision focused not on its specific holding, which too seemed uncontroversial by that point, but on the decision's doctrinal implications for challenges to laws denying homosexuals the right to marry.

Modern liberalism's attention to personal autonomy resonated broadly within the culture of late twentieth-century America. Of the trilogy "sex, drugs, and rock-and-roll," constitutional law came to give significant protection to the first and third (the latter through the First Amendment). The symbolic and perhaps even doctrinal high point of the integration of constitutional law with a culture valorizing personal autonomy may have been *Cohen v. California* (1971), where the Court, in an opinion by the strait-laced Justice John Marshall Harlan, held it unconstitutional to convict for disorderly conduct a young man protesting the war in Vietnam by displaying on the back of his jacket the phrase "Fuck the Draft." (Some justices were uncomfortable with printing the work "Fuck" in the Supreme Court Reports, and later cases invalidating similar convictions sometimes used the cosmetic "F---.")[48] On the doctrinal level, *Cohen* recognized the importance of personal autonomy when it explained why the state could not insist that Cohen use some more polite way of expressing his opposition to the draft: "One man's vulgarity is another's lyric," Justice Harlan wrote.

Occasionally scholars attempted to defend these personal-autonomy decisions in Footnote 4 terms, and in doing so revealed another source of the direct protection of personal autonomy. The reason Connecticut retained its ban on contraception, these scholars observed, was the disproportionate power of the Catholic Church in state politics.[49] More commonly, scholars defended the abortion decisions on the ground that restrictive abortion laws were implicitly discriminatory, imposing burdens on women that were not paralleled by the imposition of similar burdens on men and that resulted from the underrepresentation of women in state legislatures and from the disproportionate influence of the Catholic Church and Protestant fundamentalists in those legislatures.

These arguments were cast in the form provided by Footnote 4, but they were quite substantial extensions of the original. The arguments shifted attention from the formal characteristics of statutes defining the democratic process to the actual operation of politics in the United States. Footnote 4 was designed to license some limited judicial intervention after the collapse of classical liberal constitutional theory under the pragmatist and legal realist critiques. Shifting attention to the real world of politics would license judges to supervise public policy across an enormous range of issues. Some constitutional theorists were not dismayed by that prospect, though even they ordinarily preferred to defend judicial activism on the ground that it advanced substantive justice.

Notably, the Footnote 4 reconstruction of the personal-autonomy cases focused on what its proponents identified as the improper influence in the political process of traditionalism generally and religion specifically. Modern liberalism, with its concern for personal autonomy, was a political philosophy, translated into constitutional law, of legal elites that were increasingly secular as the century advanced. Though the association was not logically required, elite secularism was associated with opposition to the presence of religion in the making of public policy. In part, this opposition was the residue of a long-standing anti-Catholicism among Protestant elites, which diminished somewhat with the election of John F. Kennedy, but nevertheless retained a hold in the imagination of liberals and surfaced in connection with issues dealing with sexuality and reproduction. In part it was a residue as well of a similar anti-fundamentalism among elites, dating back at least to H.L. Mencken's mocking of William Jennings Bryan during the 1925 trial of John Scopes for teaching evolution, and that revived with the growing political influence of religious fundamentalists in the politics of the late twentieth century.[50]

In addition to incorporating a direct concern for personal autonomy, modern liberalism began to redefine equality in a way loosely linked to issues of autonomy, although the movement here was more halting. Classical liberalism was committed primarily to formal equality, in which legislation refrained from using what came to be known as "suspect" categories such as race, religion, and national origin. Statutes that did not use these terms could not be class legislation, because they applied to everyone equally.

Modern liberalism placed pressure on formal equality from several directions. Its proponents asked, why were only *some* classifications "suspect"? The answer they received was cast in Footnote 4 terms: when legislation allocated burdens by using these classifications, there ordinarily was reason to believe that something had gone wrong in the representative process. Modern liberals then made two moves.

First, they argued that other groups suffered the same kinds of political disadvantage. The revived women's rights movement made Footnote 4 arguments to support its claim that legislation singling out gender as a basis for allocating burdens should be treated with as much suspicion as legislation using racial classifications. Then the claims on behalf of additional groups flooded in: the poor, because their poverty disabled them from effective political participation; people with disabilities such as mental retardation, because their disabilities restricted their ability to get to the polls; gays and lesbians, because social stigmatization forced them into the closet.

The courts gradually accepted the claims made by the women's movement and, to a significantly smaller degree, those made by gays and lesbians. They resisted the claims made by persons with disabilities, but those groups made significant progress in legislation. The problem with this move was that it had no obvious limits. The political disadvantages to which modern liberals pointed were pervasive. Indeed, by the end of the century some conservatives had begun to sign on to the same arguments, but now on behalf of white ethnics, the objects of prejudice expressed, in their view, in affirmative action programs, and on behalf of small businesspeople, who could not effectively resist the power of big business and labor to obtain regulations that forced small businesses into bankruptcy.

And second, modern liberals also argued that Footnote 4 problems did not occur in on-and-off form. Rather, they were matters of degree. Constitutional law should therefore develop more nuanced approaches to questions of equality. Justice Thurgood Marshall offered the most comprehensive alternative, a "sliding-scale" approach that took account both of the degree to which a group suffered from political disadvantage and the size and importance of the burdens placed on the group by the challenged legislation.[51]

These moves in equality theory reinforced concerns, arising at roughly the same time, that formal equality—the framework within which the moves were made—was itself an inadequate account of constitutional equality. Terminology varied: within constitutional law, the typical formulation called for achieving substantive equality; in popular media, the phrase was "equality of outcome." As the law of racial equality began to develop, advocates of racial equality could and did reasonably contend that formal and substantive equality went hand-in-hand: eliminate laws requiring racial discrimination, and equality of outcome would follow relatively quickly.

Experience proved that the easy equation of substantive equality with the practical outcome of achieving formal equality was mistaken. From mid-century on, cases and statutes proliferated that made more sense as expressions of a constitutional vision of substantive equality than of formal equality. That vision, though, was controversial, and by the end of the century formal and substantive equality had become almost entirely decoupled.

In the immediate aftermath of the New Deal transformation of constitutional law, categories for dealing with equality concerns were fluid. The Court developed the doctrine of the "public forum," which required that the government make available some of its facilities—streets and parks—to people who lacked the financial resources to disseminate their messages through other means. The doctrine rested, though only implicitly, on concern about the implications of economic inequality for free speech. The restrictive covenant cases of 1948, mentioned earlier, involved legal rules that were formally neutral, barring interracial sales of all types, but the rules were unconstitutional because of their real-world effects on racial equality.

Substantive equality eventually cropped up in many areas.

## Racial Equality

*Brown v. Board of Education* (1954) held that laws segregating students by race were unconstitutional. The remedy for such laws was obvious: eliminate race as a basis for assigning students to schools. That could have been done within a year of the decision. Instead, anticipating resistance to desegregation, the Supreme Court allowed schools to desegregate "with all deliberate speed." Yet, the Court could not acknowledge openly that it was giving Southern schools time to desegregate because it knew that they did not want to. The gap between the theory justifying *Brown* and the remedy order was eventually filled by the view that the Constitution required, not merely the desegregation that the Court's remedy order allowed states to defer, but integration, which indeed could only be accomplished gradually.

The Court confirmed the shift from desegregation to integration in *Green v. School Board of New Kent County* (1968). There it said that the time for deliberate speed had ended, and that school boards were required to develop plans that "promise[d] realistically to work, and promise[d] realistically to work *now*." The only account that makes sense of the term "work" is one requiring integration.[52]

## Affirmative Action

Never constitutionally mandated, programs of affirmative action adopted by legislatures, school boards, and universities also sought to achieve substantive outcomes—in general, allocation of government benefits in proportion to the racial composition of the relevant population. Applying doctrines of formal equality, the Supreme Court whittled away at justifications that expressly invoked concern for substantive equality. By the end of the century, it seemed as if the only justification left was "diversity," a concept applicable in some settings such as education but not obviously applicable in others such as government contracting. Yet, even as the Court erected higher and higher barriers to affirmative action, such programs had enough legislative and executive support to stagger on.

Affirmative action programs brought out the connection between substantive equality and accommodation. Until the Supreme Court ruled them out, the most straightforward explanations for affirmative action were that such programs adjusted the present-day allocation of government controlled resources to rectify the continuing effects of past discrimination by governments, and that they did so to offset the effects of ongoing societal discrimination. These explanations rest on the observation that the beneficiaries of affirmative action come to the programs with material resources and human capital endowments that make them less able to take advantage of the programs than others. That in turn implies that affirmative action is a mechanism for accommodating the programs to the endowments people bring to them.

## Explicit Accommodation Requirements

By the 1980s, the proposition that equality required that institutions adjust their prior operations to make the operations fully available was firmly embedded in the law. The first appearance of the language of accommodation seems to be in the employment discrimination provisions of the Civil Rights Act of 1964. The statute's provisions on religious discrimination required that employers make "reasonable accommodations" for their employees' religious practices. Once the idea of accommodation entered the law, it spread. Employers were required to make accommodations to deal with pregnancies and with employees' needs to care for close relatives. Employers and public agencies had to make reasonable accommodations in their operations for persons with disabilities.

Relatively early in its development of the law of free exercise of religion, the Supreme Court indicated that the Free Exercise Clause required governments to adjust their programs to take account of religious practices. In 1963, it held that the clause was violated by a state law denying unemployment compensation to a person whose religious beliefs made it impossible for her to accept work on Saturday, the only work available to her in her locality (*Sherbert v. Verner*). The Court rapidly retreated from the widest implications of this holding, and eventually returned to the idea that, in the context of religious practice, the Constitution required only formal neutrality (*Employment Division v. Smith*, 1991). But, if accommodation, like its cousin affirmative action, was not constitutionally required, it could be mandated by statute (*Corporation of Presiding Bishop v. Amos*, 1987). Indeed, unlike affirmative action with respect to race, which was limited by the invocation of the idea that formal equality barred the use of race as a classifying device except in extremely unusual circumstances, accommodation in the context of religion relatively easily overcame the constitutional barrier that might have been posed by the nonestablishment principle. In general, the Court construed statutory requirements of "reasonable" accommodation rather narrowly. Some degree of substantive equality was nonetheless required once accommodation was required to any extent.[53]

Finally, the development of an accommodation-focused account of equality fit comfortably with the rise of identity politics. In one view, the entire point of identity politics was to achieve accommodations in public policy to the distinctive characteristics of identity-based groups, such as multiculturalism and multilingualism in education. Opponents of identity politics understood the point when they characterized as multiculturalists as seeking "special rights."

Substantive equality was a controversial account of constitutional equality. The political and moral valence of accommodations varied. They were largely positive when invoked in cases involving disability and age discrimination, negative in affirmative action cases. Accommodations could be expensive, and identity politics threatened the vision some held of a culturally unitary United States. In addition, substantive equality was the guiding theory of social democracy, always weak in the United States. In paying attention to the actual distribution of social goods, substantive equality immediately raised questions about the interaction between the laws structuring market transactions and the laws seeking to alter the outcome of results reached through such transactions. In the end, substantive equality could not be a theory about regulatory or redistributive laws alone; it had to be a theory about markets as well. The political support for such a theory was weak in the United States.[54]

Yet, by the end of the twentieth century no significant alternative to modern liberalism was on the scene. For a brief period in the 1980s and 1990s, it seemed as if communitarian (in the legal academy, sometimes called republican) constitutional theory might either displace or significantly limit modern liberalism. Building on a base in moral and political philosophy, communitarians argued that modern—and even classical—liberalism overlooked the important contributions society made to individual well-being, and placed too much value on individual self-satisfaction, too little on sensible constraints imposed by society in the service of long-term social stability.[55]

The communitarian impulse rapidly faded, though. Among the reasons was that communitarianism tended to accept the legal doctrines, particularly the idea of balancing interests, that modern liberalism had already come to terms with. For that reason it seemed less distinctive as a method of rights analysis than its proponents claimed; communitarians, it seemed, simply disagreed with more standard liberals on the content of the rights that should be recognized, and did not offer something truly different in kind. In addition, some rights associated with personal autonomy were so widely accepted that communitarians could not credibly reject them, and yet their political and constitutional theory left them without resources to explain how those rights could fit within a communitarian framework.

Nor did the resurgence of fundamentalist religion pose a serious challenge to the conceptual basis of modern liberalism. There was an elective affinity between modern liberalism's ideal of personal autonomy and Protestant fundamentalism's ideal of a personal relationship with Jesus Christ: both ideals worked from the inside out. In the constitutional domain, liberalism was so strong that those who sought to advance religion in the public sphere regularly relied on liberal rights-based arguments. Denying them access to public places to proselytize, for example, was said to violate the right to free speech as interpreted in standard liberal doctrine.[56] Placing statutes under a cloud merely because many of their proponents invoked religious arguments to explain why the statutes should be adopted was an even greater inroad on ordinary free speech ideas. Public financial support for parents who wanted to send their children to religiously affiliated schools, it was argued, was required so that those parents would be treated equally—substantively equally, note—to parents who could afford to make that choice by paying tuition from their personal resources.[57]

## Conclusion: Constitutional Rights at Century's End

By the end of the twentieth century, rights-based constitutionalism centered on the courts had essentially no serious competitors in the United States. Statutes protecting rights were important in large part because they elicited judicial intervention. Overturning a series of Supreme Court decisions restricting the scope of national anti-discrimination law, Congress enacted the Civil Rights Restoration Act of 1991. The term "restoration" signaled the centrality of courts to the rights-based constitutionalism at the end of the century. Statutes were important as well because they sometimes led to the creation of bureaucracies in the executive branch and in corporations that took their mission to be the vindication of the rights created by the statutes. Even here, though, the bureaucrats' mission had purchase on the larger organization because they were operating within a culture in which judicial enforcement of other rights gave rights claims an aura of presumptive legitimacy.

Rights-based constitutionalism had no necessary political valence, though. Modern liberalism was layered on to classical liberalism. Not only could conservatives call on classical liberalism to defend their positions and challenge their opponents' (as indeed could liberals), but even more, modern liberalism could be given conservative as well as liberal interpretations. Conservative constitutional theorists attacked affirmative action programs on several grounds. For example: such programs violated requirements of formal equality, true, but they also were inconsistent with the achievement of substantive equality by "white ethnics," a point specifically made by Justice Antonin Scalia, himself an Italian American.[58]

Conservative constitutional theory offered what turned out to be a supplement to modern liberalism's attention to autonomy. Conservatives argued—more in their polemics than in their judicial practice—that constitutional interpretation should rest on the original understandings of the Constitution's terms. Originalism became attractive because many of the Warren Court's innovations were not, and could not plausibly be, connected to original understandings. Warren Court decisions on criminal procedure, for example, were often expressly rooted in nontextual concerns about fairness under modern circumstances, and originalism offered an understandable alternative method to support opposition to the Warren Court's substantive results. Yet the pull of precedent and the attractions of interpretive flexibility meant that conservative judges were no more consistently committed to originalism as an exclusive method of interpretation than were their adversaries opposed to originalism.[59]

What was absent at the end of the twentieth century was a serious constitutional theory giving priority to what in the Catholic tradition was called "the common good." At most, the common good was what was left over after individual rights, both liberal and conservative, had been respected. Given the sweep of liberal and conservative claims about rights, the domain left to the common good was small indeed.

That domain could have been larger, had an earlier tradition, in which rights protection occurred outside the courts, remained vibrant. The most important institutional development over the course of the twentieth century, though, was the near disappearance of that tradition.

# *Institutions*

*L*ike constitutional ideas, the institutions of constitutional law change—slowly, sometimes randomly, and always leaving a residue that continues to affect the development of constitutional law. The focus here is on three institutions associated with the twentieth century rights revolution.

❖ The first is what political scientist Charles Epp calls the support structure for rights claims: the lawyers who put rights claims forward, and the organizations that finance them.[60] Here the story is of organizational innovation and imitation, and of political conflicts within the institutions supporting the rights revolutions.

❖ The second are the political parties, and groups within them, that find political advantage, either against the opposing party or within their own party, in supporting rights claims. Here the story is of the way in which the rights revolution assisted in the transformation of the two dominant political parties.

❖ The third are the institutions for articulating and vindicating constitutional rights. Here, the story is of a dramatic shift in institutional energy, from a world in which legislatures played a significant role relative to courts, to one in which courts were overwhelmingly dominant.

## Lawyers and Rights Litigation: The Development of Support Structures

Prior to the twentieth century, lawsuits were occasionally used to advance innovative positions on constitutional rights. Advocates of women's rights, for example, used a test-case strategy to argue, unsuccessfully, that the Fourteenth Amendment guaranteed women the right to vote.[61] *Plessy v. Ferguson* resulted from outrage among New Orleans's community of *gens du couleur*—the city's middle class community of African Americans with white ancestry—who organized a group specifically to support a challenge to the state's Jim Crow law, hired a lawyer, and recruited Homer Plessy to become the plaintiff whose case would be carried, again unsuccessfully, to the Supreme Court.[62]

---

Beginning as an organization to support draft resisters during World War I, the American Civil Liberties Union (ACLU) took on the defense of free speech for left-wing activists in the 1920s. The ACLU had a "legal committee" operating out of its national office, but at first did not directly represent defendants. The legal committee screened requests for assistance. It sent those it found worth supporting to volunteer lawyers closer to the ground, usually in the area where the case arose. Although it articulated a general vision of free speech, most of the ACLU's efforts through the 1960s were on behalf of people on the left, largely because the free speech rights most under assault were those of leftists. Nonetheless, the ACLU self-consciously refrained from defending the rights of Nazi sympathizers before and during World War II, and was quite ambivalent about the free speech rights of Communists during the early years of the Cold War. In 1940, for example, the ACLU's directors dismissed Elizabeth Gurley Flynn from its board because of her leadership role in the Communist party.[63]

A conceptual innovation occurred early in the twentieth century, although the innovative device was lost to historical memory and had to be reinvented independently two decades later. Earlier test case litigation, and the ensuing activities of the ACLU, were generally defensive—that is, constitutional challenges were raised only when the government took action against the litigants—and focused solely on the outcome of the case at hand. A group of management lawyers shifted from defense to offense, and from episodic litigation to sustained litigation with relatively long-term goals. Seeking to use the courts as a defense against labor organizing, employers supported systematic efforts by lawyers to use common law rules to bar strikes, to get the courts to construe antitrust laws to cover worker-organized boycotts, and to obtain rulings that state laws supporting labor unions by making it illegal for employers to insist that their employees not join unions were unconstitutional.[64]

These "lawyers against labor" were largely successful. But perhaps because their successes came just as classical liberalism was losing hold in constitutional law, the importance of the innovation was not immediately appreciated. The National Association for the Advancement of Colored People (NAACP), founded in 1909, had a legal department from its early years. At the start, the NAACP had a single lawyer on the organization's payroll, and used the ACLU model—which developed at the same time—of relying on lawyers in local communities who had independent legal practices and contributed their efforts to the NAACP. Unlike the ACLU's volunteer lawyers, though, the NAACP's local counsel typically received a modest fee, in light of the usually tight economic conditions of their legal practices.[65]

At first, the NAACP's lawyers adopted the defensive posture. In the mid-1920s, though, the possibility of gaining foundation support for a broader litigation effort opened up when the NAACP's chief executive, James Weldon Johnson, was invited to serve on the board of directors for a left-leaning foundation, the American Fund for Public Service. Overcoming some skepticism from other members of the board, including Roger Baldwin of the ACLU, who doubted that litigation was a promising route to success for the left, Johnson persuaded the board to promise the NAACP a substantial grant to support planning for a sustained litigation campaign against Jim Crow, and then to support the litigation campaign itself.

With the first installment of the grant in hand, the NAACP hired Nathan Margold, a recent graduate of Harvard Law School, to develop a plan. Margold's report, which became legendary within the NAACP and eventually beyond, was overly ambitious, but contained the seeds of an important perception: segregation could be undermined step by step. Margold's vision was that litigation could force southern school systems to live up to the insistence in *Plessy v. Ferguson* and later cases that segregated facilities had to be equal, and that the cost of maintaining two separate but truly equal school systems would eventually be so large as to induce the South to abandon segregation. When Margold left the NAACP to join the New Deal, the organization hired Charles Hamilton Houston, academic dean at Howard Law School and a mentor to a generation of civil rights lawyers, to continue the campaign.

Houston transformed Margold's plan in three ways, two intentionally and one the product of circumstance. Houston realized that the NAACP did not have the resources to support the kinds of direct challenges to overall inequalities in funding that Margold targeted. Instead, Houston narrowed the focus to two classes of cases. Perhaps because of his own experience as an educator in a professional school, Houston sought out cases challenging the exclusion of African Americans from state graduate and professional schools. These cases were also quite easy to frame legally, although more difficult logistically than Houston thought they would be. The legal theory was simple. Southern states simply did not provide graduate and professional educations for African Americans. Instead of "separate but equal," there was nothing at all. With the exception of one minor procedural setback, the NAACP won every Supreme Court case on graduate and professional education it brought.

Houston's second innovation was to use litigation as a means of organization building. Again he selected a target that was relatively easy legally—salaries for the African American teachers in segregated schools, which were universally lower than the salaries for white teachers of equivalent training and experience. Houston encouraged teachers, who would benefit from winning lawsuits, to join the NAACP and strengthen it organizationally. Over a period extending from the mid-1930s to the mid-1940s, the salary equalization effort was largely successful, although its effectiveness diminished once the NAACP had won the cases it brought in the South's urban areas and then turned to the much more numerous rural districts.

Houston's logistical problems led to the third change in the program of strategic litigation. It turned out that lining up plaintiffs was more difficult than Margold and Houston had thought it would be. They began with the model of defensive cases in hand, then sought to turn it around. But in defensive cases the litigants were automatically available, as defendants. Affirmative litigation required recruiting plaintiffs. Not only were there some modest ethical limits on what lawyers could do to locate potential plaintiffs, but such plaintiffs faced serious social pressure against suing. Some were fired from their jobs; others found the delays attendant on litigation too great to hold their lives in suspense awaiting a final court decision. The result was a disjuncture between the official account of the NAACP's litigation campaign—as a systematic and incremental challenge to segregation, in which one case followed logically from its predecessor eating away at segregation's foundations—and the reality of much more catch-as-catch-can litigation.

The official account prevailed in the legal imagination, though. The reason was *Brown v. Board of Education*. Looking back from 1954, lawyers saw a series of NAACP Supreme Court cases: one in 1938 holding unconstitutional Missouri's failure to provide a law school for its African American citizens (*Missouri ex rel. Gaines v. Canada*, 1938), one in 1948 extending that holding to Oklahoma (*Sipuel v. Board of Regents*, 1948), and two in 1950 holding unconstitutional Texas's effort to create a separate-but-equal law school (*Sweatt v. Painter*, 1950) and Oklahoma's creation of a special seating program for an African American seeking a graduate degree in education (*McLaurin v. Oklahoma State Regents*, 1950). In *Brown,* the Court observed that these decisions had undermined *Plessy*'s premises. In the NAACP's official account, that had been their point all along.[66]

Defensive litigation persisted, and even took on an enhanced role during the civil rights and antiwar movements of the 1960s. But the vision of affirmative and strategic litigation became central to the institutional culture of rights. The idea that lawyers, consulting and to some extent influenced by social movements, could sit down and write out a plan of litigation that, once implemented, would achieve the movements' rights-based goals, was certainly seductive to the lawyers, and the cultural power of *Brown* meant that the movements themselves were captivated, sometimes fleetingly and sometimes in the longer term, by the same idea. The vision of strategic litigation did not even require that the lawyers have the discipline of pre-existing clients or a social movement. So, for example, some aspects of the prisoners' rights movement were almost entirely lawyer developed and driven.

Staff levels at civil rights and civil liberties organizations gradually crept upwards. The ACLU created "projects" within the organization, some dedicated to strategic litigation. The NAACP and its spin-off, the NAACP Legal Defense and Education Fund (LDF), more modestly developed internal specializations and a division of labor, with the NAACP concentrating on school segregation in the North and employment discrimination, and the LDF focusing on southern segregation. New rights-oriented groups sprang up.

Strategic litigation in the late twentieth century shared the characteristics of the initial efforts. Strategic plans also were sometimes thwarted by circumstances. For example, Ruth Bader Ginsburg as director of the ACLU's Women's Rights Project envisioned creating substantial constitutional protection for women's rights by extending to women the doctrine, applicable in the context of race, that discrimination on the basis of sex was generally "suspect." She believed that judges would be more sympathetic to that argument if they were presented with cases in which the sex classification could easily be seen as disadvantaging men. She accumulated a portfolio of cases to bring to the Supreme Court. One leading possibility disappeared when Congress eliminated the sex-based classification. Meanwhile, a lawyer in Idaho involved in an ordinary family-law dispute got the first modern sex discrimination case to the Supreme Court. Sally Reed and her estranged husband were at loggerheads over who had the right to administer the tiny estate of their teenaged son, whose suicide Sally attributed to her husband's mistreatment. The ACLU had no control over this case, which resulted in a more limited holding than Ginsburg would have hoped for. She was able to recover, though, and the next cases she brought to the Court involved discrimination that could be presented as being against men. The doctrine she sought gradually worked its way into the law, culminating in a decision, written by Justice Ginsburg herself, invalidating Virginia's effort to operate "separate but equal" so-called "leadership programs" for men at the Virginia Military Institute and for women at a nearby college (*United States v. Virginia*, 1996). Notably, Ginsburg's litigation was a project of the ACLU, not of an organization distinctively associated with the modern women's movement.[67]

The welfare rights movement had a legal strategy developed in coordination with the movement's leadership. Richard Cloward and Frances Fox Piven, two New York sociologists who were students of the welfare system, observed that many poor people were eligible for specific public assistance benefits that they did not claim. They argued that the welfare community should pursue two strategies: flood the system with claims for benefits that were guaranteed by statute, and support litigation aimed at extending these statutory guarantees. Cloward and Piven were not primarily concerned about vindicating the existing statutory rights themselves. In some ways they resembled Margold: they believed that they could bring about the financial collapse of the existing welfare system and thereby provoke politicians to replace it with one that provided better guarantees of social welfare rights. And, like Margold, they overestimated what law could do. Many of the statutory challenges were successful, most notably a challenge to a common rule that a woman could not receive public assistance if there was a "man in the house" (*King v. Smith*, 1968). But statutes could be repealed—and they were. The only defense against such repeals would be a constitutional right to public assistance. Here, though, the welfare rights litigators were completely unsuccessful (*Dandridge v. Williams*, 1970). With no right to welfare hanging over their heads, legislators could maintain the specific entitlements but cut back on their size, thereby defeating the "bust the budget" strategy Cloward and Piven advanced.[68]

By the late 1960s and continuing through the end of the century, a substantial public interest bar existed to support the kinds of rights claims asserted by political liberals. It took longer for conservatives to develop a parallel structure, because the possibilities for conservative successes arose later.[69] In 1971, Lewis F. Powell wrote a memorandum to a friend at the U.S. Chamber of Commerce urging the business community to create institutions to challenge what Powell described as the domination of the left in the academy and in the "public interest" bar. The business community's first effort was a false start. The Pacific Legal Foundation, the first conservative public interest law firm, was established in 1973. Several others followed on soon after. This first group of public interest law firms achieved some modest successes, but relatively few. The reason was that they were dominated by business interests. They could not effectively present themselves as representing the public interest under those conditions. And the business community was often divided over the merits of many government programs. Some businesses—typically, large ones—benefited from government regulations that helped organize their markets and made it difficult for smaller competitors to achieve a foothold.

Conservative public interest law came into its own when it broke free from direct support from the business community and, like its liberal counterparts, began to be funded by conservative-leaning foundations. The most effective conservative public interest law firms revived classical liberal constitutional theory with its libertarian leanings. Their difficulty was that their successes—in limiting egregious environmental and small business regulations, for example—were too narrow to have much effect. They could induce the courts to strike down regulations that were quite difficult to defend, and they could invoke libertarian constitutional theories that had some potential for doctrinal expansion in doing so. But the regulatory state was so entrenched by the end of the twentieth century that these doctrines could not expand much.[70]

Changes in social movement organization and the funding sources for court-focused legal activities increased the independence of lawyers from external control. Sometimes this autonomy reinforced the social movements' achievements. Legislative victories led to the creation of bureaucracies in the executive branch and the private sector staffed by lawyers whose commitment to the rule of law led them to advance the movement's goals independent of any immediate political or financial gains to their employers. For example, the Department of Justice during the Eisenhower administration was as strongly committed to *Brown v. Board of Education* as it could have been, within the limits of political possibility, even though Eisenhower himself and many of his political advisers were unsympathetic to that decision and saw it as something that might help the Republican Party gain some ground in the segregated South. The Department of Justice's position was fueled partly by the fact that its leadership—Herbert Brownell, William Rogers, and Simon Sobeloff—came from the party's northeastern wing, which was generally liberal on issues of race. These leaders, though, used rule-of-law rhetoric to overcome political objections to their support for civil rights. As noted earlier, these lawyers worked in a legal culture that already valorized rights claims as such, and thereby validated the view that the rule of law itself called for protecting specific rights.

In other settings, the lawyers' autonomy transformed what the social movements they were affiliated with were able to achieve. When a person had to become actively engaged in some movement activity—demonstrate on the streets, or go to meetings—to be part of a social movement, lawyers had to be concerned that these activists might turn their attention inwards, and insist that the lawyers do the activists' bidding. When social movements became "checkbook" organizations, where membership consisted of writing a check every once in a while, the organizations' staffs, including their legal staffs, were much more free to follow their own inclinations. The lawyers' independence could cause difficulties.

Two episodes illustrate what the increasing autonomy of lawyers from movement control meant.

❖ The NAACP Legal Defense Fund handled the desegregation case in Atlanta, Georgia, for many years. Eventually, the local African American community, acting through the NAACP branch, decided that it would be better to abandon efforts to achieve racial balance in the increasingly black Atlanta schools, and turn instead to obtaining control over educational programming in those schools. Going around the lawyers who were nominally representing the community, local activists negotiated a settlement with the Atlanta school board that gave African American principals and teachers substantially more control over the educational programs and budgets than they had had earlier. The LDF's lawyers, strongly committed to integration, regarded the settlement as a sell-out of fundamental principles; Atlanta's activists regarded the LDF's lawyers as out of touch with the community.[71]

❖ Lawyers for the Christian Right often represented groups who were excluded from public venues otherwise available to community groups—school auditoriums outside of class time, for example. They could have used at least two legal theories to challenge the exclusion. One would have invoked the Free Exercise Clause, and would argue that the exclusions prevented religious believers from pursuing the course dictated by their religious beliefs. This theory focused on the religious nature of the activities. The other theory invoked the Free Speech Clause, arguing that the exclusions were impermissible because they were based on the content of the speech the groups planned to make and so, like all other content-based exclusions, could be justified only in unusual circumstances, never present in these cases. This theory treated religious speech simply as a subcategory of speech generally, and made nothing special about the religious content of the speech.[72]

Given the state of the law in the 1980s and 1990s, litigators for the Christian Right found it much easier to frame them as free speech cases. Yet, in doing so, they annoyed at least some of their supposed constituents, who regarded the distinctively religious component of the activities as what really mattered. The lawyers nonetheless fought the cases on free speech grounds, and won.

Social movements and foundations are inconstant sources of funding. What matters to social movements changes as they succeed in part or fail in part. Ensuring rights is sometimes, but only sometimes, important to them, and when it is not, their support for lawyers will decline. The NAACP's lawyers dominated the organization for roughly a decade, between 1945 and 1955. They were displaced by ministers in the civil rights movement of the late 1950s and 1960s, and never recovered their place in the movement. Foundations typically look for visible payoffs. They may support a project until it achieves a large success or a dramatic failure, then move on to something else. Still, by the end of the century, there was certainly a permanent baseline of support for lawyers seeking to enforce rights.

The government also provided support for rights claims.[73] One might think this unlikely, because rights claims are asserted against the government. Why would a government provide resources to challenge its own programs? The reasons vary. Sometimes the national government had an interest in challenging state and local governments; sometimes the Constitution was interpreted to require the government to do so; and sometimes government support for particular constitutional challenges unintentionally generated political support for a broader examination of other policies or programs.

In the early 1940s, the Department of Justice created a Civil Rights Section, whose purpose was to enforce the relatively few existing criminal laws against violations of civil rights. These laws prohibited violent interferences with exercises of constitutional rights. Lacking enthusiasm and the political capital for the enactment of a federal law against lynching, the Roosevelt administration created the Civil Rights Section as a way of addressing lynchings in the South. The section gradually grew, and was converted into a full-fledged "division" within the department by the Civil Rights Act of 1957. Over the next decades, the division's responsibilities expanded to include enforcement of voting rights laws, anti-discrimination laws, and more. Here the national government intervened to enforce civil rights guarantees against state and local governments.[74]

Starting in the 1930s, the Supreme Court held that some criminal defendants were entitled to legal representation at public expense. At the outset, as in the Scottsboro cases, representation was provided by the private bar, with lawyers with general practices occasionally representing clients whose fees were paid by the government. Gradually, larger cities adopted public defender systems where the only services the lawyers provided were to those unable to afford private representation. The expansion of legal services of this sort was fueled by the Supreme Court's decision in 1963 that every defendant facing substantial time in jail if convicted was entitled to a lawyer (*Gideon v. Wainwright*, 1963).[75]

The expansion of public defender services had a collateral, and largely unintended, effect. Working for the poor became attractive, and possible, for many new graduates of law schools in the 1960s. Although the Supreme Court did not interpret the Constitution to require that litigants involved in civil cases have representation except in extremely limited circumstances, the ideas of justice that could be drawn from the criminal representation cases provided reasons for politicians to support the creation of legal services programs with civil components. The national Legal Services Corporation, created in 1974, provided federal funds to neighborhood legal services groups, which provided legal assistance in cases involving housing, welfare benefits, and more.

Lying on the boundary between public and private support for rights-based litigation are rules authorizing the courts to require that a defendant who loses pay the attorneys' fees incurred by the winning plaintiff. After the Supreme Court held that the federal courts did not have the power to award such attorneys' fees routinely, Congress intervened and enacted a statute authorizing the courts to do so in civil rights cases.[76] The statute helped place some forms of rights-based litigation on a reasonably firm financial basis, allowing lawyers to make a living as civil rights lawyers.

The limitations on the private sector of the support structure have parallels for the public sector. Obviously, public institutions have only the resources they get from politicians. And, structurally, the activities of legal services groups and the Civil Rights Division inevitably provoke political opposition. Enforcement priorities vary as administrations change. One administration may gain more political support than it loses by vigorously enforcing voting rights; its successor may decide that enforcing other anti-discrimination laws provides greater political benefits. Funding levels vary with the political climate. In 1996, Congress placed substantial limits on the types of representation that could be provided by groups that received funding from the Legal Services Corporation. Their lawyers could not bring class action suits, for example, nor could they participate in desegregation litigation. They could represent individuals seeking public assistance benefits, but—in a provision the Supreme Court held unconstitutional—Congress attempted to bar legal services attorneys from raising constitutional challenges to the denial of a benefit to a client (*Legal Services Corporation v. Velazquez*, 2001). A limited reaction set in as well to the provision of attorneys' fees in civil rights cases, with Congress cutting back on the availability of attorneys' fees awards only in cases involving attempts by prisoners to vindicate their constitutional rights.[77] Conservatives sometimes spoke of a broad program of "defunding the left," but their successes were relatively limited.[78]

Despite the limitations on private and public support for rights-oriented organizations, by century's end the organizations had become a seemingly permanent part of the structure of rights protection in the United States. What mattered was not whether they would exist, but how robust they would be, and how they would interact with each other and with the rest of the political system.

## Political Parties and Social Movements

Constitutional law provides the structure in which politics occurs, but it also figures in the strategies political parties adopt. Social movements can threaten to disrupt existing party structures as insurgencies within one party or as vehicles of social disorder that make an opposition party's claim that it can restore order credible.[79] Political leaders respond to these difficulties by attempting to incorporate the social movements' ideals, and then some elements of the movements themselves, into their political agendas. A platform plank on a constitutional issue can reach out to voters; an administration policy position dealing with constitutional rights can appeal to a constituency within the party or undermine the position taken by the administration's opponents either in the party or outside it. Notably, this is likely to occur on both sides of the political aisle. What may differ between the parties is not their willingness to seek support from a constituency interested in a particular rights claim, but rather the particular way in which the parties—or, more precisely, leaders within the parties—accommodate the rights claim in policy proposals that fit comfortably within their party's broader approach to public policy.[80] Politicians thereby build new visions of the Constitution into politics.

The reaction to what Progressives saw as the excesses of *Lochner*-ism gave the pragmatic critique of rights political content by reviving long-standing arguments that courts should rarely intervene to overturn democratically enacted legislation in the name of ill-defined constitutional rights. As noted earlier, in the 1920s Felix Frankfurter called for repealing the Fourteenth Amendment's Due Process Clause because it had become a license for wide-ranging judicial interference with political outcomes. Eventually politicians began to call this a theory of "judicial restraint."

Politicians who think they have a good chance of winning in popular arenas but not in judicial ones favor judicial restraint. Once they gain control of the courts as well—which happens if they prevail long enough in ordinary electoral politics—their concerns shift. They then ask, how can we use constitutional rights to our political advantage? The Footnote 4 jurisprudence developed during the New Deal provided the answers for a generation.

❖ Footnote 4 told the courts to refrain from invoking the Constitution to question the policy choices at the New Deal's heart. The New Deal's regulatory initiatives, which to some extent deprived the New Deal's opponents of financial resources that they could use to oppose the New Deal and to some extent built support for the Democratic Party among businesses that benefited from the market organization created by New Deal policies, would be untouched by the courts.

❖ Franklin Roosevelt's nominations to the Supreme Court were dictated by his insistence that only those who supported core New Deal programs be appointed.[81] An unintended effect of this requirement was that the pool of potential nominees was rich with men who were generally liberal on issues of civil rights and civil liberties. These appointees, and their decisions, solidified support for the Democratic Party among centrist liberals. Their decisions on issues of race began to pull African Americans away from the Republican Party, although the New Deal's economic policies clearly played a larger role.

❖ Roosevelt's New Deal faced opposition from conservative southerners within the Democratic Party. Roosevelt failed in his efforts to displace them directly by supporting their challengers within the party. He turned, only somewhat consciously, to using a rights strategy to undermine their power. The Civil Rights Section took them on, by supporting constitutional challenges to primary elections in which only white party members were eligible to vote. These initiatives promised payoffs in the long rather than the short term, both in the displacement of Roosevelt's opponents and, again, in the attraction of African Americans to the party. They offset the administration's failure to support anti-lynching legislation, and, notably, demonstrated the administration's good faith on issues of race not only to African Americans in the jurisdictions where white primaries were held but to African

Americans in the North, a constituency that became increasingly important to the Democratic Party as rural African Americans migrated during World War II and after to the urban North.

The rights revolution played a smaller role in the reconciliation of the Republican Party to the New Deal brought about by Dwight Eisenhower. Particularly after *Brown v. Board of Education*, Eisenhower's political advisors understood the possibilities for Republican gains in the South. Yet, civil rights policy remained in the hands of more traditional Republicans such as Herbert Brownell and William Rogers, both of whom were prominent New York lawyers before they joined the Eisenhower administration, and Simon Sobeloff, who served as solicitor general at a critical time, who continued to see their party as Abraham Lincoln's party. Republicans did not capitalize on the difficulties *Brown* created for the Democratic Party until the 1960s.

The McCarthy wing of the Republican Party took advantage of Cold War concerns about national security to attack Democrats for their associations with communists. The Warren Court's reaction was initially tepid, then more vigorous. The Roosevelt appointees who remained on the Court tried to use the First Amendment and the Fifth Amendment to shield so-called "fellow travelers" from legal assault, and by the end of the 1950s were joined by enough others to provide some degree of constitutional cover for Democrats against McCarthy-like charges. Unlike the "southern strategy," here the Republican effort to turn the rights revolution against Democrats failed almost completely.

Political parties were one of the main mechanisms by which social movements contributed to the rights revolution. Movements motivate their members in part by the ideals they offer. Sometimes judges and legislators are directly moved by the ideals as well, but more often politicians see the social movements as a source of political support (or, sometimes, as a bad influence on society that they can point to in order to gain political support from the movement's opponents). They fold the movements' ideals into their political platforms. Democrats signed on to the constitutional visions offered by the civil rights movement of the 1950s and 1960s, and by the feminist movement of the 1970s and 1980s. The environmental movement's concerns had not crystallized as rights based by the end of the twentieth century, but Democratic politicians and some Republican ones—notably, Richard Nixon—saw political advantages to becoming environmentalists. If the civil rights movement influenced the Democratic Party's commitment to rights, the reaction to that movement and to the Warren Court's decisions on prayer in the public schools generated the Christian Right social movement that shaped the Republican Party's commitment to a different set of rights.[82]

These examples show how the rights revolution could benefit or harm the major political parties seen as coalitions, and their constituent elements. This was perhaps even more dramatic during the 1960s and 1970s, when the Warren Court's support for modern liberalism, coupled with congressional civil rights initiatives, simultaneously enhanced the position of modern liberals within the Democratic Party and weakened the party's support in more traditional venues, including the South. The effect is captured in the comment Lyndon Johnson reportedly made on signing the Civil Rights Act of 1964: "There goes the South for a generation,"[83] meaning, "There goes southern support for the Democratic Party." Johnson's commitment to civil rights was both principled and political. As he saw it, northern liberals, mainly urban and including many African Americans, were a more important component of the party coalition than the southern conservatives who, Johnson accurately predicted, would sooner or later lose their seats to a resurgent Republican Party in the South.

The Warren Court shaped the Republican Party in another way. Its decisions expanding constitutional rights in criminal proceedings occurred just as crime rates increased dramatically. Richard Nixon campaigned for the presidency as a law-and-order candidate who would reshape the Supreme Court by appointing justices who would support what Nixon called the forces of peace rather than the forces of disorder.[84]

As with the Progressive attack on the *Lochner* Court, the Republican challenge to the Warren Court initially took the form of advocacy of a general theory of judicial restraint. The Warren Court had gone wrong, Republicans contended, by interfering with the policies elected representatives endorsed. And, as with the Progressives, this was a theory that worked as long as its advocates controlled legislatures but not the courts. As Republican appointees came to dominate the courts, the rhetoric of judicial restraint became less attractive, although it never entirely lost its hold.

The reason is that the United States experienced an extended period of divided government at the end of the twentieth century. Republicans controlled the presidency for twenty of the twenty-four years between 1969 and 1993, and only Republicans nominated Supreme Court justices during that period because no vacancies occurred during Jimmy Carter's presidency. But Democrats controlled Congress during the entire period (except for six years when Republicans had a majority in the Senate but not the House of Representatives). From a political point of view, what Republicans needed was a constitutional theory that *supported* judicial intervention when their political adversaries prevailed politically. A general posture of judicial restraint would not do.

Republicans solved their problem by insisting that the courts could intervene when—but only when—legislation was inconsistent with constitutional provisions as they were understood at the time they were adopted.[85] Departing from an interpretive tradition in which original understanding figured as one among many bases for constitutional interpretation, the constitutional theory of the Republican Party at the end of the twentieth century was almost exclusively originalist. Judicial restraint mattered, within originalist accounts, only when the original understanding supported restraint; judicial restraint was a category within originalist theory, not the principle that should always guide constitutional interpretation.

Like the Footnote 4 jurisprudence it replaced, at least among Republicans, originalism was sufficiently flexible to do the political jobs for which it was used. Outside the domain of constitutional rights, for example, Republicans—believing that their control of the presidency was likely to extend into the indefinite future—relied on originalist arguments to support expansive views of presidential power largely free from congressional control. Scholars might argue that Republicans deployed originalism selectively or used originalist sources opportunistically. The Republican small business constituency, for example, found environmental and related land-use regulations bothersome. Republican constitutional theorists responded by developing the argument that oppressive regulations might constitute a "taking" of property without the compensation required by the Constitution. Scholars responded that nothing in the original understanding supported that position. But, with some tweaking of the evidence, the Supreme Court's takings decisions could be re-presented as sufficiently originalist to satisfy their constitutional theory,

By the 1980s and 1990s, Republicans had also become committed to vigorous protection of free speech across a rather broad range—certainly broader than free speech protection in 1791. They argued that commercial speech deserved the same degree of protection that political speech did, and challenged campaign finance regulations on free speech grounds. These arguments were straightforwardly doctrinal, not originalist, and conservative constitutionalists made few attempts to defend them in those terms. Conservative interpretive theory reproduced the eclecticism of its liberal counterpart, with perhaps a modest twist, in which the components of eclectic interpretation were allocated to different theorists instead of being part of everyone's toolkit.

This and other difficulties with originalism did not weaken it as the prevailing interpretive theory for the Republican Party. Here public education played a large role. From the New Deal on, those who wrote about the Constitution and the Supreme Court in the popular press wavered between the view that courts should be restrained and the view that courts should promote justice, both of which were parts of the New Deal's constitutional legacy. The latter position came to dominate during the 1960s and 1970s, although the former continued to have its advocates. Republican publicists mounted a sustained campaign of public education, whose effect was to make it the conventional wisdom that constitutional interpretation had to be originalist.

Even liberals bought into originalism, at least to the extent that they tried to defeat conservative originalists on originalist grounds. Liberals argued, for example, that conservatives could defend the proposition that affirmative action was inconsistent with the Constitution as originally understood only if they described the original understanding on a rather high level of generality. But, liberals said, on that level of generality, the Constitution as originally understood also supported a right to privacy of a sort that was anathema to conservatives.

Divided government persisted through the end of the twentieth century.[86] In those circumstances, the political uses of constitutional rights would inevitably be confused. Democrats defended a constitutional right to choice with respect to abortion because women committed to the right to choose had become an important constituency within the party. Republicans challenged the constitutionality of affirmative action programs because white men who believed themselves to be disadvantaged by affirmative action had become an important constituency within *that* party. Divided government made fights over constitutional rights increasingly intense.

## From Congress to the Courts: The Venues for Rights Protection

The American discourse of rights underwent a substantial institutional reallocation during the twentieth century. In part because of the typically defensive nature of rights assertions, and in part because of the institutional thinness of the support structure of rights assertions in courts, the language of rights was widely used in ordinary political discourse—in addition, of course, to being deployed in courts. Outside the courts, though, the lawyer's conceptual structures—the division of rights into three categories, for example—played a much smaller role. Advocates of the rights of labor, in the labor movement or in progressive political circles, were uninterested in determining whether the rights of labor were civil or social rights. They were, simply, rights. If they could be secured in the courts, well and good, but securing them through legislation was just as good—and seemingly easier.

The growth of the support structure began a process of change. The ACLU and the NAACP both started out interested as much in influencing legislation and educating the public about their rights concerns as in winning court cases. The ACLU rapidly and the NAACP more gradually began to focus on courts. The federal income tax law restricted lobbying by organizations that received donations exempt from taxation, but that was only a minor reason for the shift. The more important one was that the organizations could almost never win anything in the legislature or through influencing executive officials, but could occasionally win something in the courts. The Palmer Raids of the 1920s showed the ACLU that it had no influence on the executive branch; the NAACP's repeated failures to obtain anti-lynching legislation from a New Deal Congress controlled by Democrats, because of the strategic positions occupied by conservative Southern Democrats, taught it the same lesson.

One should not exaggerate the rate at which rights were in fact protected by the courts, but getting something from them was better for the organizations, and for rights, than getting nothing from legislatures. In a political version of Say's Law—the (questionable) economic theory that supply elicits demand—successes in courts gave lawyers increasing prominence within the communities interested in rights, and this made it easier for the lawyers to assert that their activities deserved an increasing share of the funds available for all rights-oriented activities. Here too the institutional thickening of the support structure made lawyers who focused on the courts a group within each organization and social movement whose interests had to be accommodated.

The content of the rights courts protected, compared to the rights of labor and the like, also affected the shift of resources into the courts. Courts were good at protecting rights that fit easily into a classical liberal framework, such as rights to free expression and equality understood in formal terms. The courts could reverse convictions for making assertedly dangerous speeches, or direct executive officials to refrain from enforcing statutes that discriminated on the basis of race. Through most of the twentieth century the remedies available for violations of rights that swept more broadly—roughly speaking, second-generation rights to social and economic well-being, and third-generation rights to a desirable physical and cultural environment—were not well-developed. What law professor Abram Chayes called public law litigation emerged in the late twentieth century with remedies aimed at forcing public bureaucracies to reform and behave in a constitutionally acceptable manner.[87] The reign of public law remedies was relatively brief, though. Not surprisingly, there was a strong political backlash against public law remedies, leading to the adoption of legislation such as the Prison Litigation Reform Act that sharply limited the remedies courts had used to bring prisons into line.

Protecting rights to economic well-being faced another obstacle. Nearly everyone agreed that the best way to secure such rights was through legislation, with courts playing a secondary role. The best justifications for such rights were found in the social democratic tradition. That tradition had vaguely, and sometimes not so vaguely, Marxist overtones, and its strongest purveyor in the United States in the 1930s was the Communist Party. Civil libertarians were properly suspicious of getting too closely aligned with communists, partly because of a justified concern that such an association would impair their ability to gain public support for their *other* concerns because of "Red-baiting," and partly because of an equally justified concern that communist leaders hoped to turn independent organizations into the party's agents.

The Scottsboro cases provided an early and bitter lesson to the NAACP. A communist-front organization wrested control over the cases from the NAACP through a public relations campaign that damaged the NAACP's image among many of its most important supporters, charging the NAACP's lawyers with failing to provide a sufficiently vigorous defense to the nine African Americans who were being railroaded to death. Afterwards, the NAACP's leaders were chary of anything that had even a slight tinge of communist influence. Younger activists in the NAACP forced the leadership to convene a conference in 1933, at which the Young Turks insisted that the organization devote greater attention to labor organizing as a means of advancing the interests of working-class African Americans. The leadership went along with the demand half-heartedly, but, strikingly, its main activities with respect to labor unions in the 1940s involved legal challenges to various rules that excluded African American workers from unions.[88]

As law professor Risa Goluboff has shown, civil rights lawyers in the 1940s, inside the government and in the NAACP, saw the possibility of constructing an ideal of civil rights in which economic security played a large role.[89] They chose a different path, partly because the precedents with which they had to work made it easier to develop a race-related ideal than an economic security one, and partly because they worried that the association of economic security with unions and, in particular, the Communist Party would limit what they could achieve with respect to economic security and, even more, impair their overall efforts with respect to racial equality.

Interest in protecting economic well-being as a right enjoyed a brief revival in the late 1960s, but this time almost exclusively through efforts to obtain judicial rulings that the Constitution protected such a right. Occasionally advocates would push legislation forward with rhetoric like, "health care is a human right," but far more commonly they supported their proposals as good social policy, not as the implementation of a right. In the final quarter of the century, Congress enacted a large number of statutes dealing with environmental protection. Each was defended as good social policy. Near the end of the century, environmental activists looked back at their accomplishments, and began to describe what they sought—a decent environment—as a human right. Environmental legislation also began to produce judicial remedies that were more nuanced than the traditional injunction, even the public law structural injunction. But these developments at their incipient stages when the twenty-first century began, and whether they would spread, in the environmental field or beyond, remained unclear.[90]

Until the rise of a jurisprudence of accommodation and substantive equality, the very discourse of rights suggested that rights could only be vindicated in court. The discourse was one of *individual* rights, but achieving something in other venues—whether in the culture, the streets, or legislatures—required coordinated group action. The few late twentieth-century critics of the culture of rights focused on the way the discourse of rights seemed inevitably to separate people from each other.[91] With the development of a new jurisprudence of equality, resort to venues other than the courts became increasingly plausible, although the hold of individualist ideas of rights was so strong that arguments *against* use of the courts seemed out of touch with institutional reality.[92]

Social movements did not abandon legislatures, of course. They sought, and sometimes obtained, rights-protective statutes. And, while an important feature of such statutes was that they provided remedies in courts for rights violations, the statutes—or perhaps more precisely the mobilization that secured their enactment—sometimes helped change social understandings about the practices the statutes made unlawful. On the liberal side, statutes like the Family and Medical Leave Act (1993) reinforced the sense that women and men should share duties of family caretaking; on the conservative side, state legislation restricting the power of cities to condemn property for purposes of economic development reinforced the sense that people's homes were particularly important to them. Describing these statutes disparagingly as merely symbolic because few people actually enforced the rights they created understates their importance in contributing to a culture of rights. And, once the laws were on the books, the common view that people ought to do what the law says helped reshape social understandings about the rights the statutes protected. Legislatures, then, did not fall completely out of the picture. Nonetheless, their role was smaller, relative to the courts', at the end of the century than it had been at its outset.

One thing overshadowed all these discrete points: *Brown v. Board of Education*. There the Supreme Court had faced up to the greatest challenge to the proposition that the U.S. Constitution was an instrument of justice, and by holding Jim Crow laws unconstitutional lodged rights protection almost unshakably within the courts. Congress and the presidency, even when controlled by political liberals, had failed to do anything significant about Jim Crow. The Supreme Court did. That the Court's follow-through after *Brown* was shaky, and that the Court's actions on their own did little to bring about real desegregation, which occurred when the civil rights movement pushed Congress to enact the civil rights statutes of the 1960s, mattered little for the cultural authority the Court eventually garnered from what it had done in *Brown*. *Brown* brought into focus all the blurry ideas about rights and how courts could vindicate them that entered the legal culture after 1937 without being systematized. The Court's triumph in *Brown* sharply limited the availability within U.S. culture of alternative venues for vindicating rights.

# Conclusion: Into the Twenty First Century

**W**here will the rights revolution go in the twenty first century? First, and perhaps most important, ideas never die. Everything that the rights revolution made available to discussions of rights remains available for the future—older ideas about rights as well as newer ones. And older ones might come to displace the newer ones: accommodations and "special rights" might come to be understood as inconsistent with equality properly understood as limited to formal equality. The mechanisms would involve social movements and political parties, but the ideas would have their own integrity. One result is that by the turn of the century more problems were posed as implicating competing rights claims rather than posing a rights claim against a social interest or public policy. That in turn had two effects. The rhetorical power of invoking rights diminished, though of course it did not disappear. More important, the method for resolving conflicts changed. Rights could be trumps, in Ronald Dworkin's terms, when they were posed against policies or interests. Posed against other rights, though, they had to be balanced. And, as argued probably most clearly by Richard Posner, balancing rights against rights amounts to a pragmatic instrumentalism on the level of rights, which too weakens the rhetorical value of an appeal to rights.[93]

The institutional thickening seems as permanent a part of the national political system as lobbyists and interest groups. Globalization has changed the general institutional environment of the ordinary practice of law. Family lawyers in Tulsa, Oklahoma, deal with international law—the Hague Convention on the Civil Aspects of Child Abduction—when, as they inevitably will, they must deal with a custody dispute between a U.S. resident and her European or Asian spouse who has returned "home" with the family's children. Commercial lawyers in Tulsa deal with international law when they buy and sell oil and gas in transactions with Russian and British corporations. International law has begun to insinuate itself into rights litigation, with a large accompanying controversy.[94] The support structure of legal rights has already expanded somewhat to include transnational nongovernmental organizations such as Amnesty International. As legal practice globalizes, the invocation of international norms in rights litigation may come to seem more natural than it does today.

For much of the second half of the twentieth century the United States was the focal point of the world's attention to rights. The Warren Court became the model for a rights-protecting court, and the rights revolution in general seemed to have advanced further in the United States. By the end of the century the picture had changed. The rise of conservative politics in the United States, and the retreat from Warren Court jurisprudence in the Supreme Court, moved the United States from the center to the periphery of worldwide rights discourse. Judges and scholars began to look for insights on rights and how to elaborate them to the European Court on Human Rights, the German Constitutional Court, and the Constitutional Court of South Africa, and often used the United States as an example of how *not* to protect rights. In the twenty-first century, the United States may well be just one nation doing valuable things with rights, and perhaps not the most important one.

Institutionally, courts will probably continue to dominate. Some innovations in the form of judicial review, sometimes influenced by reflection on experience with judicial review in other nations, open space for a more vigorous assertion of rights in legislatures, through what some describe as a dialogue between courts and legislatures about rights, and what others characterize as a distinctive, "experimentalist" form of judicial review. The possibility of a constitutional crisis on the order of the one that occurred in 1937 cannot be ruled out, either. In that event, popular constitutionalism might regain some of its attractiveness.

The connection between ideas and social movements makes forecasting questionable, because we can never know which social movements will generate ideas that politicians will find useful vehicles for their ambition. At the moment the most vibrant movements are the Christian Right and the gay rights movement, but whether they will remain vibrant, and whether they will disappear or be supplemented by some other movements—animal rights?—is unknowable. And so, therefore, is the future of the rights revolution.

# *Suggestions for Further Reading*

or a prominent but controversial general theoretical account of constitutionalism and judicial review, see John Hart Ely, *Democracy and Distrust: A Theory of Judicial Review* (Cambridge, Mass.: Harvard University Press, 1980). For an account of developments in theories of constitutional interpretation, see Johnathan O'Neill, *Originalism in American Law and Politics: A Constitutional History* (Baltimore: Johns Hopkins University Press, 2005).

For general accounts of the U.S. Supreme Court and constitutional rights decisions during the mid-twentieth century, see Lucas A. Powe, *The Warren Court and American Politics* (Cambridge, Mass.: Harvard University Press, 2000); Morton Horwitz, *The Warren Court and the Pursuit of Justice* (New York: Hill and Wang, 1999); and William Wiecek, *The Birth of the Modern Constitution: The United States Supreme Court, 1941–53* (New York: Cambridge University Press, 2006).

For general histories of rights in America, see David Hackett Fischer, *Liberty and Freedom: A Visual History of America's Founding Ideas* (New York: Oxford University Press, 2005); and Eric Foner, *The Story of American Freedom* (New York: W.W. Norton, 1999). Some accounts of specific rights include Risa Goluboff, *The Lost Promise of Civil Rights* (Cambridge, Mass.: Harvard University Press, 2007); Michael Klarman, *From Jim Crow to Civil Rights: The Supreme Court and the Struggle for Racial Equality* (New York: Oxford University Press, 2004); Alexander Keyssar, *The Right to Vote: The Contested History of Democracy in the United States* (New York: Basic Books, 2001); Howard Gillman, *The Constitution Besieged: The Rise and Demise of Lochner Era Police Powers Jurisprudence* (Durham, N.C.: Duke University Press, 1993); David E. Bernstein, "Lochner's Legacy's Legacy," *Texas Law Review* 92 (2002): 1; Mark A. Graber, *Transforming Free Speech: The Ambiguous Legacy of Civil Libertarianism* (Berkeley: University of California Press, 1992); David Rabban, *Free Speech in Its Forgotten Years* (New York:

Cambridge University Press, 1997); John C. Jeffries and James E. Ryan, "A Political History of the Establishment Clause," *Michigan Law Review* 100 (2001): 279; and David Garrow, *Liberty and Sexuality: The Right to Privacy and the Making of* Roe v. Wade (Berkeley: University of California Press, 1998).

On lawyers and rights litigation, see Mark Tushnet, *The NAACP's Legal Strategy against Segregated Education, 1925–50*, rev. ed. (Chapel Hill: University of North Carolina Press, 2004); Steven Teles, *The Rise of the Conservative Legal Movement: The Battle for Control of the Law* (Princeton, N.J.: Princeton University Press, 2008); Daniel Ernst, *Lawyers against Labor: From Individual Rights to Corporate Liberalism* (Urbana: University of Illinois Press, 1995); Charles R. Epp, *The Rights Revolution: Lawyers, Activists, and Supreme Court in Comparative Perspective* (Chicago: University of Chicago Press, 1998); Samuel Walker, *In Defense of American Liberties: A History of the ACLU* (Carbondale: Southern Illinois University Press, 1999); and Martha Davis, *Brutal Need: Lawyers and the Welfare Rights Movement, 1960–73* (New Haven, Conn.: Yale University Press, 1993).

# *Notes*

1. For a discussion of *Miranda* in popular culture, see Susan Bandes and Jack Beerman, "Lawyering Up," *Green Bag* 2d 2, no. 5 (1998).

2. *Lochner v. New York*, 198 U.S. 45 (1905); *Griswold v. Connecticut*, 381 U.S. 479 (1965).

3. *Plessy v. Ferguson*, 163 U.S. 537 (1896).

4. Daniel R. Ernst, *Lawyers against Labor: From Individual Rights to Corporate Liberalism* (Urbana: University of Illinois Press, 1995).

5. Sometimes it is useful to think of this group more narrowly as an interest group. With respect to most aspects of the argument here, nothing analytically important turns on whether we describe the group as a social movement or an interest group. I suspect that leaders of relatively narrow interest groups have to do somewhat more work to develop a rights-based defense of their claims than do leaders of social movements, but I am confident that they can do so and have sometimes done so.

6. As I suggested at the outset, appeals to rights have a particular valence in U.S. political culture, and so can—although they need not always—serve as a more effective rhetoric for mobilizing support than appeals to "mere" interests. When social movement leaders make their strategic choices, rhetoric is one dimension of choice, and sometimes they will choose the rhetoric of rights.

7. Here I rely on the insights of Reva Siegel and Robert Post. See, for example, Siegel, "Constitutional Culture, Social Movement Conflict, and Constitutional Change: The Case of the De Facto ERA," *California Law Review* 94 (2006): 1323; Seigel and Post, "Popular Constitutionalism, Departmentalism, and Judicial Supremacy," *California Law Review* 92 (2004): 1027.

8. For a conceptualization of the ways in which changing ideas and institutions overlap, see the discussion of "intercurrence" in Karen Orren and Stephen Skowronek, "Institutions and Intercurrence: Theory Building in the Fullness of Time," in *NOMOS 38: Political Order*, ed. Ian Shapiro and Russell Hardin (New York: New York University Press, 1996).

9. Rebecca J. Scott, "Public Rights, Social Equality, and the Conceptual Roots of the *Plessy* Challenge," *Michigan Law Review* 106 (2008): 777.

10. For a discussion, see Mark V. Tushnet, "Political Aspects of the Changing Meaning of Equality in Constitutional Law: The Equal Protection Clause, Dr. Du Bois, and Charles Hamilton Houston," *Journal of American History* 74 (1987): 884.

11. See generally Howard Gillman, *The Constitution Besieged: The Rise and Demise of Lochner Era Police Powers Jurisprudence* (Durham, N.C.: Duke University Press, 1993).

12. 163 U.S. 537, 552 (1896).

13. 169 U.S. 366, 397 (1898).

14. 198 U.S. 45 (1905).

15. 208 U.S. 412, 422 (1908).

16. 245 U.S. 60, 74–75 (1917).

17. 262 U.S. 390, 401, 399 (1923).

18. For a discussion, see David E. Bernstein, "Lochner's Legacy's Legacy," *Texas Law Review* 92 (2003): 1.

19. Mark Graber, *Transforming Free Speech: The Ambiguous Legacy of Civil Libertarianism* (Berkeley: University of California Press, 1992); David Rabban, *Free Speech in Its Forgotten Years* (New York: Cambridge University Press, 1997).

20. On *Buchanan* as a libertarian decision, see David E. Bernstein, "Philip Sober Controlling Philip Drunk: *Buchanan v. Warley* in Historical Perspective," *Vanderbilt Law Review* 51 (1998): 797.

21. William E. Forbath, *Law and the Shaping of the American Labor Movement* (Cambridge, Mass.: Harvard University Press, 1991), 1–2n3.

22. Samuel Gompers, "Judicial Vindication of Labor's Claims," *American Federationist* 7 (1901): 283, 284.

23. See generally Forbath, *Law and the Shaping of the American Labor Movement.*

24. Rabban, *Free Speech in Its Forgotten Years,* 184 (describing the connection between Roscoe Pound's sociological jurisprudence and pragmatism).

25. John Dewey, "The Social Possibilities of War," quoted in David Kennedy, *Over Here: The First World War and American Society*, 50 (New York: Oxford University Press, 1980); Rabban, *Free Speech in Its Forgotten Years*, 246, 184–89 (Pound's letter is quoted at 189).

26. For a discussion of the Progressive commitment to affirmative government action in aid of liberty, see Eric Foner, *The Story of American Freedom* (New York: W.W. Norton, 1999), 152–55.

27. Foner, *Story of American Freedom*, 140.

28. Foner, *Story of American Freedom*, 178.

29. See, for example, "The Red Terror of Judicial Reform," *The New Republic* (October 1, 1924): 110 (unsigned but written by Frankfurter).

30. 208 U.S. 420 (1908).

31. Arthur F. Bentley, *The Process of Government: A Study of Social Pressures* (Chicago: University of Chicago Press, 1908).

32. See generally Walter Rauschenbusch, *Christianity and the Social Crisis* (New York: Macmillan, 1907); John A. Ryan, *Distributive Justice: The Right and Wrong of Our Current System of Wealth* (New York: Macmillan, 1916).

33. Robert L. Hale, "Coercion and Distribution in a Supposedly Non-Coercive State," *Political Science Quarterly* 38 (1923): 470, 478.

34. *Corrigan v. Buckley*, 271 U.S. 323 (1926); *Shelley v. Kraemer*, 334 U.S. 1 (1948).

35. Martin Shapiro, "Fathers and Sons: The Court, the Commentators, and the Search for Values," in *The Burger Court: The Counterrevolution That Wasn't*, ed. Vince Blasi (New Haven, Conn.: Yale University Press, 1983).

36. 304 U.S. 144 (1938).

37. *West Coast Hotel v. Parrish*, 300 U.S. 379, 399 (1937).

38. *Colegrove v. Green*, 328 U.S. 549 (1946).

39. Technically, one might respond to this criticism by noting that the legislature drawing Illinois's congressional district lines was not itself under challenge as malapportioned. Still, Frankfurter and his colleagues clearly understand that Frankfurter intended his analysis to extend to all apportionment cases: "The policy with respect to federal elections does mean that

state legislatures must make real effort to bring about approximately equal representation of citizens in Congress. Here the legislature of Illinois has not done so." 328 U.S. 572 (Black, J., dissenting).

40. *Powell v. Alabama*, 287 U.S. 45 (1932); *Gideon v. Wainwright*, 372 U.S. 335 (1963); *Norris v. Alabama*, 587 (1935).

41. *Chambers v. Florida*, 309 U.S. 227, 241 (1940).

42. Bruce Ackerman, "Beyond Carolene Products," *Harvard Law Review* 98 (1985): 713.

43. Cass R. Sunstein, *The Second Bill of Rights: FDR's Unfinished Revolution and Why We Need It More than Ever* (New York: Basic Books, 2004).

44. See Note, "A Brooding Omnipresence: Totalitarianism in Postwar Constitutional Thought," *Yale Law Journal* 106 (1996): 423.

45. *McLaughlin v. Florida*, 379 U.S. 184 (1964); *Loving v. Virginia*, 388 U.S. 1 (1967).

46. 381 U.S. 479 (1965).

47. 539 U.S. 558 (2003).

48. *Cohen v. California*, 403 U.S. 15 (1971); *Rosenfeld v. New Jersey*, 408 U.S. 901 (1972); *Lewis v. New Orleans*, 415 U.S. 130 (1974).

49. See, for example, David Garrow, *Liberty and Sexuality: The Right of Privacy and the Making of* Roe v. Wade (Berkeley: University of California Press, 1998), 113–16, 127–28.

50. See generally John C. Jeffries and James E. Ryan, "A Political History of the Establishment Clause," *Michigan Law Review* 100 (2001): 279.

51. *Dandridge v. Williams*, 397 U.S. 471, 521 (Marshall, J., dissenting).

52. 391 U.S. 430, 439 (1968).

53. *Sherbert v. Verner*, 374 U.S. 398 (1963); *Employment Division v. Smith*, 494 U.S. 872 (1990); *Corporation of Presiding Bishop v. Amos*, 483 U.S. 327 (1987).

54. One indication of the difficulties associated with an explicit theory of substantive equality is the short story "Harrison Bergeron" by Kurt Vonnegut, a person whose political sympathies were clearly to the left of

center, offering a critique of substantive equality that was frequently cited by those to the right of center. Kurt Vonnegut, "Harrison Bergeron," in *Welcome to the Monkey House* (New York: Dell, 1968). For a conservative use of the reference, see *PGA Tour, Inc. v. Martin*, 532 U.S. 661, 705 (2001) (Scalia, J., dissenting).

55. The resources available at the web site of the Communitarian Network provide a good introduction to communitarian ideas, www.gwu.edu/~ccps/index.html.

56. *Capitol Square Review Board v. Pinette*, 515 U.S. 753 (1995).

57. For an argument to this effect, see Clint Bolick, *Voucher Wars: Waging the Battle over School Choice* (Washington, D.C.: Cato Institute, 2003).

58. See, e.g., Antonin Scalia, "The Disease as Cure: 'In Order to Get Beyond Racism, We Must Take into Account of Race,'" *Washington University Law Quarterly* (1979): 147.

59. For a discussion, see Mark Tushnet, "The United States: Eclecticism in the Service of Pragmatism," in *Interpreting Constitutions: A Comparative Study*, ed. Jeffrey Goldsworthy (Oxford: Oxford University Press, 2006).

60. Charles R. Epp, *The Rights Revolution: Lawyers, Activists, and Supreme Court in Comparative Perspective* (Chicago: University of Chicago Press, 1998).

61. See *Minor v. Happersett*, 88 U.S. 162 (1875).

62. Charles A. Lofgren, *The* Plessy *Case: A Legal-Historical Interpretation* (New York: Oxford University Press, 1988), 29–41.

63. Samuel Walker, *In Defense of American Liberties: A History of the ACLU* (Carbondale: Southern Illinois University Press, 1999), 132-33.

64. Ernst, *Lawyers against Labor*.

65. See Mark Tushnet, *The NAACP's Legal Strategy against Segregated Education, 1925–50*, rev. ed.) (Chapel Hill: University of North Carolina Press, 2004).

66. *Missouri ex rel. Gaines v. Canada*, 305 U.S. 337 (1938); *Sipuel v. Board of Regents*, 332 U.S. 631 (1948); *Sweatt v. Painter*, 339 U.S. 629 (1950); *McLaurin v. Oklahoma State Regents*, 339 U.S. 637 (1950).

67. See Philippa Strum, *Women in the Barracks: The VMI Case and Equal Rights* (Lawrence: University Press of Kansas, 2004), 59–60.

68. *King v. Smith*, 392 U.S. 309 (1968); *Dandridge v. Williams*, 397 U.S. 471 (1970); Frances Fox Piven and Richard Cloward, *Poor Peoples' Movements: Why They Succeed and How They Fail* (New York: Pantheon Books, 1977); Martha Davis, *Brutal Need: Lawyers and the Welfare Rights Movement, 1960–73* (New Haven, Conn.: Yale University Press, 1993).

69. For a good overview, see Steven Teles, *The Rise of the Conservative Legal Movement: The Battle for Control of the Law* (Princeton, N.J.: Princeton University Press, 2008).

70. Conservative public interest lawyers were not the only ones seeking to develop a set of conservative constitutional rights. As Richard Lazarus has shown, the emergence of a specialized Supreme Court bar in the late twentieth century is attributable to sustained corporate interest in eating away at the regulatory state. Richard Lazarus, "Advocacy Matters Before and Within the Supreme Court: Transforming the Court by Transforming the Bar," *Georgetown Law Journal* 96 (2008): 1487. In my view, this is the best recent example of an expansion of constitutional rights fueled by an interest group rather than by a social movement.

71. Derrick Bell, "Serving Two Masters: Integration Ideals and Client Interests in School Desegregation Litigation," *Yale Law Journal* 85 (1976): 470; Tomiko Brown-Nagin, "The Impact of Lawyer-Client Disengagement on the NAACP Legal Defense Fund's Campaign to Implement *Brown v. Board of Education*," in *From the Grassroots to the Supreme Court*, ed. Peter Lau (Durham, N.C.: Duke University Press, 2005).

72. Hans Hacker, *The Culture of Conservative Christian Litigation* (Lanham, Md: Rowman & Littlefield, 2005).

73. See Epp, *Rights Revolution*, 61–64.

74. See Risa L. Goluboff, *The Lost Promise of Civil Rights* (Cambridge, Mass.: Harvard University Press, 2007), 253–59.

75. *Gideon v. Wainwright*, 372 U.S. 335 (1963); Anthony Lewis, *Gideon's Trumpet* (New York: Vintage, 1981).

76. *Aleyska Pipeline Co. v. Wilderness Society*, 421 U.S. 240 (1975); Civil Rights Attorneys Fees Awards Act of 1976, 42 U.S.C. § 1988.

77. *Legal Services Corporation v. Velazquez*, 531 U.S. 533 (2001); Prison Litigation Reform Act, Pub. L. No. 104-134 (codified in various portions of the U.S. Code).

78. Grover Norquist, "Defunding the Left," *American Spectator* (September 1995).

79. Frances Fox Piven, *Challenging Authority: How Ordinary People Change America* (Lanham, Md.: Rowman & Littlefield, 2006), emphasizes the disruptive power of social movements, focusing on moments of large-scale disruption but also mentioning the more ordinary times of absorption of social movements into the structure of politics.

80. Focusing on a large number of income-support programs, Christopher Howard usefully emphasizes the bipartisan nature of support for such programs, and the variations in the ways in which the two major parties seek to advance income-support goals. Christopher Howard, *The Welfare State Nobody Knows: Debunking Myths about U.S. Social Policy* (Princeton, N.J.: Princeton University Press, 2007). For a discussion of the bipartisan nature of policy-making during periods of divided government, see David R. Mayhew, *Divided We Govern: Party Control, Lawmaking, and Investigations, 1946–90* (New Haven, Conn.: Yale University Press, 1991).

81. Kevin J. McMahon, *Reconsidering Roosevelt on Race: How the Presidency Paved the Road to Brown* (Chicago: University of Chicago Press, 2003).

82. For a general discussion, see William N. Eskridge Jr., "Some Effects of Identity-Based Social Movements on Constitutional Law in the Twentieth Century," *Michigan Law Review* 100 (2002): 2062.

83. For a reference to this statement, see Timothy Noah, "Forget the South, Democrats," *Slate*, January 27, 2004, http://www.slate.com/id/2094552.

84. Fred P. Graham, *The Self-Inflicted Wound* (New York: Macmillan, 1970).

85. Johnathan O'Neill, *Originalism in American Law and Politics: A Constitutional History* (Baltimore: Johns Hopkins University Press, 2005).

86. Mark Tushnet, *A Court Divided: The Rehnquist Court and the Future of Constitutional Law* (New York: Norton, 2005).

87. Abram Chayes, "The Role of the Judge in Public Law Litigation," *Harvard Law Review* 84 (1976): 1281.

88. For discussions of the organizations' problems with the Communist Party, see Wilson Record, *Race and Radicalism: The NAACP and the Communist Party in Conflict* (Ithaca, N.Y.: Cornell University Press, 1964); Walker, *In Defense of American Liberties*, 127-30, 155–56.

89. Goluboff, *Lost Promise.*

90. Richard Lazarus, *The Making of Environmental Law* (Chicago: University of Chicago Press, 2004).

91. For a representative example from the center-right, see Mary Ann Glendon, *Rights Talk: The Impoverishment of Political Discourse* (New York: Free Press, 1993); for an example from the left, see Mark Tushnet, "An Essay on Rights," *Texas Law Review* 62 (1984): 1363.

92. See especially Laurence H. Tribe, "The People Themselves: Judicial Populism," review of *The People Themselves: Popular Constitutionalism and Judicial Review*, by Larry D. Kramer, *New York Times Book Review*, October 24, 2004.

93. Richard Posner, Law, *Pragmatism, and Democracy* (Cambridge, Mass.: Harvard University Press, 2003).

94. For a discussion of the controversy, see Austen L. Parrish, "Storm in a Teacup: The U.S. Supreme Court's Use of Foreign Law," *University of Illinois Law Review* 2007 (2007): 637.